EXPLORING THE FRONTIER

A SOURCEBOOK ON THE AMERICAN WEST

EXPLORING
THE FRONTIER

A SOURCEBOOK ON THE AMERICAN WEST

Edited by Carter Smith

AMERICAN ALBUMS FROM THE COLLECTIONS OF
THE LIBRARY OF CONGRESS

THE MILLBROOK PRESS, *Brookfield, Connecticut*

Cover: "The Unknown Explorers." Painting by Frederic Remington, 1906.

Title Page: "Yosemite Valley." 1887 chromolithograph after a painting by Andrew Melrose.

Contents Page: Drawing of a horned toad, by Charles Willson Peale for the Lewis and Clark expedition, 1805.

Back Cover: "Mackenzie," painted in 1906 by Frederic Remington and published in Collier's Weekly *magazine.*

Library of Congress Cataloging-in-Publication Data

Exploring the frontier : a sourcebook on the American West / edited by Carter Smith.
    p. cm. -- (American albums from the collections of the Library of Congress)
    Includes bibliographical references and index.
    Summary: Describes and illustrates the exploration the American frontier from 1774 to the late nineteenth century, through a variety of images created during that period.
    ISBN 1-56294-128-3 [lib. bdg.]
    1. Frontier and pioneer life--United States--Juvenile literature. 2. United States--Territorial expansion--Juvenile literature. 3. United States--Discovery and exploration--Juvenile literature. 4. United States--Exploring expeditions--Juvenile literature. [1. West (U.S.)--History--Sources. 2. United States--Discovery and exploration--Sources.] I. Smith, C. Carter. II. Series.
E179.5.E96 1992
973--dc20
                                   91-31131
                                       CIP
                                       AC

Created in association with Media Projects Incorporated

C. Carter Smith, *Executive Editor*
Lelia Wardwell, *Managing Editor*
Elizabeth Prince, *Manuscript Editor*
Anne B. Wright, *Principal Writer*
Charles A. Wills, *Consulting Editor*
Kimberly Horstman, *Researcher*
Lydia Link, *Designer*
Athena Angelos, *Photo Researcher*

The consultation of Bernard F. Reilly, Jr., Head Curator of the Prints and Photographs Division of the Library of Congress, is gratefully acknowledged.

Manufactured in the United States of America.

10 9 8 7 6 5 4 3 2 1

Contents

Introduction   7

Part I: 1774–1802
A New Nation Ventures West   9

Part II: 1803–1835
The First Wave Across the Mississippi   33

Part III: 1836–1900
Charting Challenging Territory   69

Resource Guide   94

Index   95

The sheer cliffs of the Sierra Nevadas in eastern California tested the skills of the most capable explorers of the American West. Early explorers often over-looked the beauty of the region as they tried to negotiate difficult terrain. This view of the Sierras was painted by American artist Thomas Moran (1837–1926), who traveled throughout the West in the late 1800s, painting Western vistas that have become American treasures.

Introduction

EXPLORING THE FRONTIER is one of the volumes in a series published by The Millbrook Press titled AMERICAN ALBUMS FROM THE COLLECTIONS OF THE LIBRARY OF CONGRESS and the first of six books in the series subtitled SOURCEBOOKS ON THE AMERICAN WEST. They treat the history of the West from pioneer days to the early twentieth century.

The editors' goal for the series is to make available to the student many of the original visual documents of the American past which are preserved in the Library of Congress. Featured prominently in EXPLORING THE FRONTIER are the many fine editions of early nineteenth-century Western literature maintained in the Library's Rare Book and Special Collections Division and the portraits and other images of frontiersmen and explorers in the Library's Division of Prints and Photographs. The images reproduced here show the many ways in which nineteenth-century Americans saw the West and its characters.

Many Americans were first introduced to the people and scenery of the West through the illustrated expedition reports usually issued by government agencies and other supporters of these excursions. While most of the reports' illustrations were relatively dry and scientific, some notable exceptions stand out. Patrick Gass's unofficial 1807 journal of the Lewis and Clark expedition, with its crude but lively woodcuts, provided a vivid accounting of mishaps and incidents on the journey. Among the most elaborate productions in the exploration literature was Henry R. Schoolcraft's six-volume *History of the Indian Tribes of the United States*, illustrated by Seth Eastman, an artist best known for his romantic paintings of Indian life.

Of the many heroic figures of the West—the fur traders, the Long Hunters, and explorers—images of them were seldom produced during their own eras. Most of the portraits we have of California explorer John Charles Frémont, in fact, were produced during his later political career. The rare examples, like St. Memin's portrait of Meriwether Lewis, are typically naturalistic and straightforward. Like the riverboatmen of the Mississippi, these figures were relatively unsung until they were recognized by the writers and artists of the mid-nineteenth century as representatives of a vanished way of life. The men in these early portraits bear little resemblance to the explorers, trappers, and frontiersmen imaginatively illustrated for the popular histories and stories of the 1840s and 1850s by G.W. Fasel, F.O.C. Darley, and other artists.

The many works reproduced here represent a small portion of the wealth of pictorial records of Western life preserved by the Library of Congress in its role as the nation's library.

BERNARD F. REILLY, JR.

Part I: 1774–1802
A New Nation Ventures West

Daniel Boone's first attempt to lead settlers into the Kentucky wilderness ended in disaster when the party was attacked by Indians. But Boone was not deterred. In 1775, he helped cut a road through the Cumberland Gap to ease the way for settlers, and by the late 1770s, small settlements had begun to take root. Over the next twenty years, the population of what is now Kentucky would increase by more than 70,000, forcing Boone and others who sought the solitude of the wilderness to push farther west.

The boundaries of the American West were not fixed. The notion of the West was based on the frontier: the line between the westernmost fringe of white settlements and the wilderness. Although American frontiersmen pushed the boundaries and made Westward expansion possible, they were usually not the first to explore the territory into which they wandered. When American colonists began to venture across the Appalachian Mountains as early as 1740, much of the territory west of the mountains had already been explored by French and Spanish fur traders and missionaries.

American frontiersmen often crossed the mountains to escape the expensive and confining way of life in the East. Although the West provided relief, it presented its own challenges. Individuals able to meet these challenges became American legends, creating a uniquely American way of life. As settlers continued to spread west, frontiersmen moved farther into the Western wilderness. Pushing the frontier beyond the Mississippi River as the nineteenth century began, these pioneers helped shape the West.

The American government encouraged exploration, particularly of the fur-rich lands of the Pacific Northwest. Spanish, English, and Russian explorers also traveled the Pacific Coast during the later part of the eighteenth century, setting the stage for territorial conflicts faced by Western explorers over the next fifty years.

Americans were slow to venture into the Western lands they won in the Revolutionary War. Under the Treaty of Versailles in 1783, the United States received most of the territory extending from the Atlantic Coast inland to the Mississippi River. To the north, the Canadian border was fixed at its present-day point. To the south, the United States extended as far as Florida, which was retained by Spain. At the end of the war, settlers began crossing the Appalachians into what would become Ohio, Kentucky, and Tennessee. But once they arrived, they faced the threat of conflict with Indian tribes before they could claim the land as their own.

Thomas Jefferson supported American efforts to extend the nation's boundaries. He dreamed of a nation that would stretch from the Atlantic to the Pacific. The Louisiana Purchase in 1803 went a long way toward fulfilling that dream. The new territory, which doubled the size of the nation, was bounded on the east by the Mississippi River and on the west by what is now Texas, Colorado, and Idaho. American explorers would spend the next fifty years combing the territory.

The size of the country continued to increase as disputed territory and Spanish colonial holdings came into American hands. By the beginning of the Civil War, all the area we now know as the continental United States was under American control.

THE GROWTH
of the
UNITED STATES
From 1776 to 1867

The acquisitions made by the United States from
1776 to 1867 are shown by different colors.

The boundaries of the States and Territories at the close
of 1867 are outlined by solid green lines:

The Capitals of the States and Territories
in 1867 are shown on map by: ⊙

0   100   200   400   600

Scale of Miles

THE M.-N. WORKS.

A TIMELINE OF MAJOR EVENTS

PART I *1774–1802 A New Nation Ventures West*

UNITED STATES HISTORY

1776 Twelve of the thirteen colonies send delegates to Philadelphia, where they issue the Declaration of Independence.
•British General William Howe wins the Battle of Long Island, capturing New York City and White Plains, New York. General George Washington retreats.
•Washington crosses the Delaware River and defeats Hessian troops at Trenton, New Jersey.

John Paul Jones

1777 General Washington wins an important victory over the British at Princeton, New Jersey.
•The Cherokee Indians surrender all of their territory in South Carolina under the Treaty of DeWitts Corner.
•The Continental Congress authorizes a flag for the United States that will have thirteen stars and thirteen alternating red and white stripes.

1778 The Articles of Confederation are adopted by the Continental Congress.

1779 U.S. naval commander John Paul Jones wins a victory against the British frigate *Serapis* off the east coast of England.

1780 The British overrun South Carolina and capture Charleston.

1782 Benjamin Franklin, John Adams, and John Jay negotiate a peace treaty with the British.

1783 The Revolutionary War ends when the U.S. and Britain sign the Treaty of Paris.

1784 James Madison sets forth his argument for the separation of church and state

EXPLORING THE FRONTIER

1774 Spanish explorer Juan Bautista de Anza and Father Francisco Garces travel from the Santa Cruz Valley across the Colorado Desert, in search of an overland route to Monterey Bay, in what is now California.
•Spanish explorer Juan Perez becomes the first person to sail along the Pacific Coast from Mexico to what is now Washington State.

1775 Daniel Boone blazes a 300-mile trail through the Cumberland Gap, a pass through the Appalachian Mountains from North Carolina to Tennessee and Kentucky. It later becomes the Wilderness Road, a major route to the West for settlers.

1776 English explorer Captain

Frontiersman Daniel Boone

James Cook embarks on a voyage to the Pacific Northwest in search of the Northwest Passage, a northern water route that many believe will link the Atlantic and Pacific oceans.
•Spanish explorers Father Silvestre Velez de Escalante and Father Athanasio Dominguez explore and map the mountains in what is now Utah, Arizona, Colorado, and New Mexico.

in *Remonstrances Against Religious Assessments*.

1785 Thomas Jefferson becomes U.S. minister to France, and John Adams is named minister to Great Britain.

1787 Delegates from twelve of the thirteen states draft the U.S. Constitution.

1789 George Washington becomes the first president of the United States.

1790 The temporary federal capital is moved from New York City to Philadelphia.

1791 The Bill of Rights is added to the Constitution.

1792 Thomas Jefferson forms the Republican Party to oppose the Federalist Party and to represent the rights of farmers and those in favor of a less centralized government.

1792 Washington and Adams are

West Point, New York

reelected president and vice president, respectively.

1796 Federalist John Adams is elected president and Democratic-Republican Thomas Jefferson is elected vice president.

1801 *The New York Evening Post* is first published in New York City by Alexander Hamilton and John Jay.

1802 The United States Military Academy is established by Congress; it is located at West Point, New York, on the Hudson River.

1779 James Robertson leads a party along the Cumberland River in search of a place to establish a settlement. Nashborough (later Nashville) is founded at the spot chosen by Robertson.
•Juan Bautista de Anza continues his travels in the Southwest, exploring the San Luis Valley and the Arkansas River.

1784 John Filson, explorer and author, publishes a map of Kentucky,

based in part on surveys by Daniel Boone. Filson writes about Boone in his book *The Discovery, Settlement, and Present State of Kentucke*.

1785 Publication of an account of Captain Cook's journey sparks public interest in the Pacific Northwest.

1788 French Canadian Julian Dubuque is granted permission by the Fox Indians to mine lead in what is now

Iowa. He is the first white settler in the area.

1791 The British government sends George Vancouver to explore the western coast of Canada. Part of the area he explores is named after him.

1792 Nautical explorer Robert Gray discovers a river in the Pacific Northwest which he names for his ship, the *Columbia*.

1793 British explorer Alexander

Mackenzie travels across Canada to the Pacific. His overland journey is the first recorded crossing of North America.

1796 In his ship, the *Otter*, Captain Ebenezer Dorr is the first American to explore the California coastline.
•On an exploratory mission for the French government, General Victor Collot maps the Ohio River and continues down the Mississippi River to New Orleans.

THE OLD NORTHWEST

By the time of the American Revolution, French explorers and fur traders had traveled throughout the Old Northwest, in what is now Ohio, Michigan, Indiana, Illinois, and Wisconsin. French explorers had been traveling in North America since the sixteenth century, concentrating first on eastern Canada. In the early seventeenth century, Samuel de Champlain ventured south into the Great Lakes region. In 1672, Father Jacques Marquette (1637–75) joined cartographer (mapmaker) Louis Joliet (1645–1700) in an expedition in which they became the first Europeans to travel down the Mississippi River.

Explorer René Robert Cavelier, sieur de La Salle (1643–87), also explored the Great Lakes region and traveled down the Mississippi in 1680, establishing Fort Crevecoeur near the site of present-day Peoria, Illinois. By 1700, there were also French trading posts at Detroit and Green Bay in what are now Michigan and Wisconsin; St. Louis was founded by the French in 1764. But as the French moved south, the English moved west. Territorial conflicts began, resulting in the French and Indian War. The war broke the French hold on the North American interior, but French fur traders continued to travel throughout the Old Northwest.

Christopher Gist (c. 1706–59; left) was one of many surveyors sent into the wilderness by English land speculators. Gist explored the Ohio River as far west as today's Louisville, traveling through western Pennsylvania, Ohio, and Kentucky. He was the first to produce an accurate survey of northeastern Kentucky. In the engraving, Gist is returning home from Kentucky to Yadkin, North Carolina.

In 1659, Pierre Esprit Radisson (1632–1710) left Quebec and traveled by canoe (below) to what is now Wisconsin. Radisson traded directly with the Indian tribes he found in the area and made a handsome profit. He went on to ally himself with English fur traders, and formed the Hudson's Bay Company. Over the next 150 years, Hudson's Bay would lead the way west to the Pacific.

THE OLD SOUTHWEST

The region known as the Old Southwest included what is now the states of Florida, Mississippi, Alabama, Tennessee, and Kentucky. Exploration of this region was begun by the Spanish more than 200 years before American frontiersmen ever ventured south. Juan Ponce de León (1460–1521) arrived on the Florida coast in 1513, and Hernando de Soto (c.1500–42) explored areas of Georgia, Florida, Tennessee, and the Carolinas. Although permanent settlements did not take root for a number of years, Spanish exploration continued in the region throughout the sixteenth century.

As Spanish explorers and missionaries traveled in the area, conflicts often erupted with French fur traders who had traveled south from Canada. By 1700, the Spanish had established a fort at the site of present-day Pensacola, Florida, and would soon establish settlements along the Mississippi River as far north as Illinois.

The founders of St. Louis, Pierre Laclede (c. 1724–78) and his fourteen-year-old stepson, Auguste Chouteau (1749–1829), traveled up the Mississippi from New Orleans to establish the post. The family helped establish good trading relations with the Osage Indian tribe and were among the first American fur trappers to cross the Mississippi in the 1800s. This house (opposite, top) was built by Auguste Chouteau.

As increasing numbers of French, English, and American explorers pushed their way south into Spanish territory, Spain tried to make its empire more visible by setting up forts and settlements along the Mississippi River. Nogales (present-day Vicksburg, Mississippi), founded in 1793, was one of these settlements. This drawing (opposite, bottom) was made by a French explorer who traveled down the Mississippi and Ohio rivers in 1796.

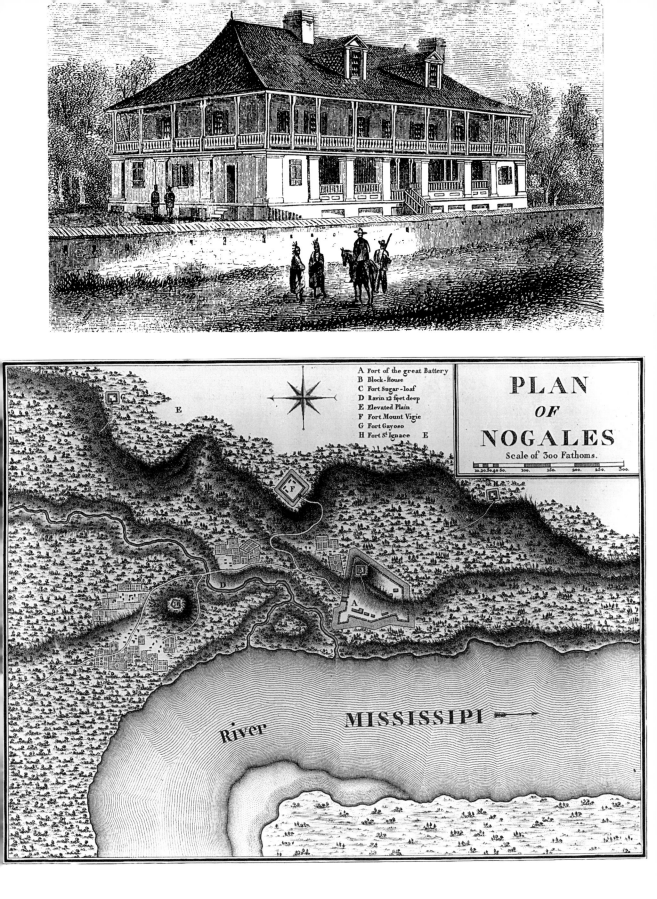

Plan of Nogales
Scale of 300 Fathoms.

A Fort of the great Battery
B Block-House
C Fort Sugar-loaf
D Ravin 12 feet deep
E Elevated Plain
F Fort Mount Vigie
G Fort Gayoso
H Fort St. Ignace

River MISSISSIPI

LONG HUNTERS

In the years before the Revolutionary War, the American frontier moved slowly across the Appalachian Mountains into what are now the states of Tennessee, Kentucky, and Ohio. Among the first white men to cross the mountains were the "Long Hunters," so called because they hunted in Western forests for months at a time to meet the demand for furs and buckskins in the East. In the process, the Long Hunters came to know the geography of the territory in detail. They would use this knowledge in the frontier battles of the Revolution, and later to guide settlers moving west.

The lives of the Long Hunters were filled with hazards and hardship. With little more than a rifle, a Long Hunter supplied himself with food, clothing, and an income besides. Indians were a constant threat, and Long Hunters learned to heed such warning signals as a broken twig or the cry of an animal. Many came to prefer this life; they relished the adventure, as well as the self-sufficiency and solitude offered by the wilderness. To preserve this way of life, Long Hunters had to push farther west as settlers followed them across the mountains. They and their descendants would continue westward, just ahead of the settlers, leading American exploration of the frontier well into the next century.

Long Hunters depended on flintlock rifles for their livelihood, protection, and food. Daniel Boone referred to his rifle as his "best-fren." Because the barrel was about forty-six inches long, these guns were known as "long rifles." Gunpowder was carried in horns like the one hanging from the rifle (right).

The ordeals endured by Simon Kenton (1755–1836) at the hands of his Indian captors made him a legend among frontiersmen (below). Captured in 1778, he was forced repeatedly to run the gauntlet and was tied to the stake three times. Kenton eventually escaped to Kentucky, where he resumed his career as a wilderness scout.

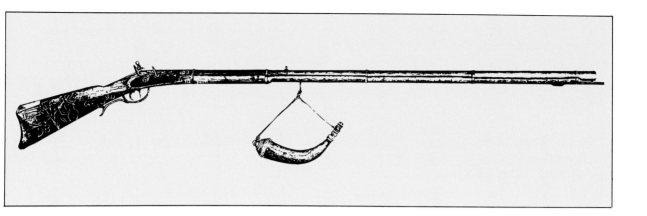

WEST TO THE MISSISSIPPI

Among the first of the Long Hunters to travel west was Benjamin Cutbird, who led a small party across the Appalachians in 1766. Cutbird and his companions hunted and trapped along what is now the Tennessee–Kentucky border until they reached the Mississippi River. They then traveled south by river to New Orleans, where they sold their catch.

Reports of abundant game and fertile soil from members of Cutbird's expedition sparked the interest of others. Simon Kenton began extensive hunting and trapping in Kentucky, as did Mike Stoner, John Finley, and John Stuart. James Knox led a party of forty hunters from Virginia to Kentucky in 1770. They explored the Green River Valley and much of western Kentucky.

In 1772, George Rogers Clark (1752–1818) made his first expedition down the Ohio River in search of fertile land. James Robertson traveled from western North Carolina to Tennessee, guiding settlers over the Smoky Mountains. He then led a group farther west along the Cumberland River to found the town that would eventually become Nashville. Many of these Long Hunters would soon put their wilderness skills to use in the Revolutionary War.

James Robertson (1742–1814; above) traveled west from North Carolina with a party of hunters in search of a place to settle. He helped to establish a settlement along the Cumberland River in 1780. His wife had taught him to read and write as an adult. Robertson used these skills as leader of the new settlement and later as Indian agent for the Cherokee tribe.

Frontiersman John Finley (left) first saw Kentucky in the 1750s, when he was captured by the Shawnee tribe. Impressed by its rich farmland and abundant game, he learned from his captors of an easy pass through the mountains into the territory. Finley returned to Kentucky with Daniel Boone, but left the expedition after Indian attacks began to plague the hunters.

DANIEL BOONE

Of all the Long Hunters, none is better known than Daniel Boone (1734–1820). Growing up in the frontier settlement of Yadkin, North Carolina, Boone acquired the skills he would need to survive in the wilderness he loved. As an adult, he spent winters hunting and trapping, each year traveling farther west.

Having heard tales of rich land and plentiful game in the region of Kentucky, Boone resolved to go there himself. He sought a route through the Cumberland Gap, a passage through the mountains of North Carolina into Kentucky. Finally, in the spring of 1769, he was able to locate the gap with John Finley. They made their way into Kentucky by way of an Indian trail called the Warriors' Path.

Boone remained in Kentucky for two years, exploring the Red and Kentucky rivers and the Green and Cumberland valleys. He returned to Kentucky on many occasions to hunt, to cut a road through the Cumberland Gap, and finally to settle. But as Kentucky became more crowded, Boone had to move farther west. He died in Missouri, having never given up the life of a Long Hunter.

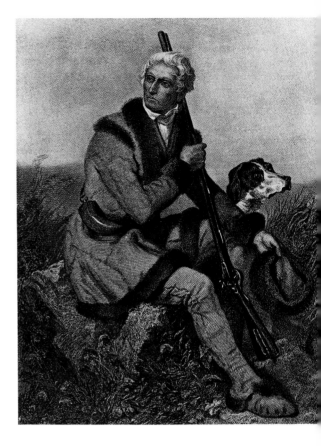

Boone (above) spent his last years in the Missouri territory, leaving Kentucky in 1798–99 as his business ventures failed. The claims he had staked to rich farmland were often improperly recorded. This meant he could not prove ownership and sell the claims as he had hoped. He died in Missouri at the home of his son in 1820.

This lithograph (below) illustrates Daniel Boone's rescue of his daughter, Jemina, and her companions, who were kidnapped by Indians when they wandered to a river near Boonesborough. Two of his sons, James and Israel, were killed by Indians: Israel died in a battle against Indians who were attacking a settlement during the Revolutionary War, and James was ambushed along a trail while returning with supplies.

EIGHTEENTH CENTURY SPANISH EXPLORATION IN THE SOUTHWEST

The Spanish had explored and settled much of Mexico and parts of what is now Arizona and New Mexico. But they did not settle California until the mid-eighteenth century. At that time, Russian explorers, moving along the Pacific Coast in Northern California, threatened Spanish control of the area. In response, José de Galvez, governor of the Spanish territory, quickly assembled an expedition under Father Junípero Serra, a Franciscan missionary, and explorer Gaspar de Portolá.

In the spring of 1769, the party set out from northern Mexico on a 400-mile trek over unexplored desert and winding mountain paths. They reached San Diego on July 1 and quickly built a mission station. Portolá and some of his men then continued north in search of a large, deep, sheltered bay that had been described by Spanish explorers over a century before. The party crossed the Santa Lucia Mountains with some difficulty, reaching the Monterey Bay. It proved to be a shallow, open inlet, so they traveled on. After abandoning hope of locating the bay, the party decided to return to San Diego. Making their way back by a slightly different route, Portolá's scouts discovered the San Francisco Bay, the deep sheltered arm of the Pacific they had come north to find.

THE EXPEDITION INTO CALIFORNIA
OF THE VENERABLE PADRE FRAY

Junípero Serra

AND HIS COMPANIONS IN THE YEAR 1769

as told by Fray Francisco Palóu

AND HITHERTO UNPUBLISHED LETTERS OF SERRA
PALÓU AND GALVÉZ: THE WHOLE NEWLY TRANSLATED AND
ARRANGED AS A CONSECUTIVE NARRATIVE WITH
THE AID OF THOMAS W. TEMPLE II

By Douglas S. Watson.

TO WHICH IS ADDED THE ACCOUNT OF
SERRA'S DEATH INSCRIBED BY FRAY FRANCISCO PALÓU IN THE
BOOK OF THE DEAD AT CARMEL MISSION

Printed at the Nueva California Press: San Francisco 1934

Father Junípero Serra (1713–84) left his native Spain to become a missionary in 1749. Serra founded nine missions in California, beginning with San Diego in 1769. Until his death in 1784, he traveled often among the missions and into the interior of California. An account of his expedition into California (above) was recorded in 1769.

Russian explorers were moving steadily south from Alaska to Northern California in the 1700s in search of new sources of sea otter pelts and meat and grain for their more northern outposts. Indians from the San Jose mission, south of San Francisco Bay, perform a tribal dance (below) for a Russian exploring party.

SPANISH MISSIONS

The mission settlements established by Portolá and other Spanish explorers were not self-sustaining. In order to obtain the goods they needed, a new supply route from Mexico had to be found. An expedition was formed in 1774 under Spanish explorer Juan Bautista de Anza and Franciscan missionary Father Francisco Garces.

The expedition ran out of supplies on its first attempt to cross the desert and turned back. On the second attempt, the group managed to cross the Coropa Mountains and the San Jacinto Mountains. By March they arrived at their long-awaited destination, the San Gabriel Mission. They were back in Tubac by May, having traveled 3,000 miles.

Over the next several years, de Anza led other expeditions to California, establishing missions and settlements. Missionaries, such as Fransciscan friars Silvestre Velez de Escalante and Franscisco Athanasio Dominguez, created trails throughout the Southwest. Many of these trails were abandoned as Spanish influence in the Southwest declined. Fifty years later they were rediscovered by Mexican and American explorers, at the height of the Santa Fe Trade.

This map (above), showing the Pacific coastline from the 48th to the 50th parallel, is based on observations by Spanish naval explorers Alejandro Malaspina and Francisco Eliza. Malaspina was sent by the Spanish in 1789 to study the Pacific Coast. Eliza explored the Pacific Northwest, in search of sites for Spanish settlement.

The California missions (right) established in the late 1700s were a joint effort of the Spanish government and the Catholic Church. Indians were brought to live at the missions to receive religious instruction and work mission farms.

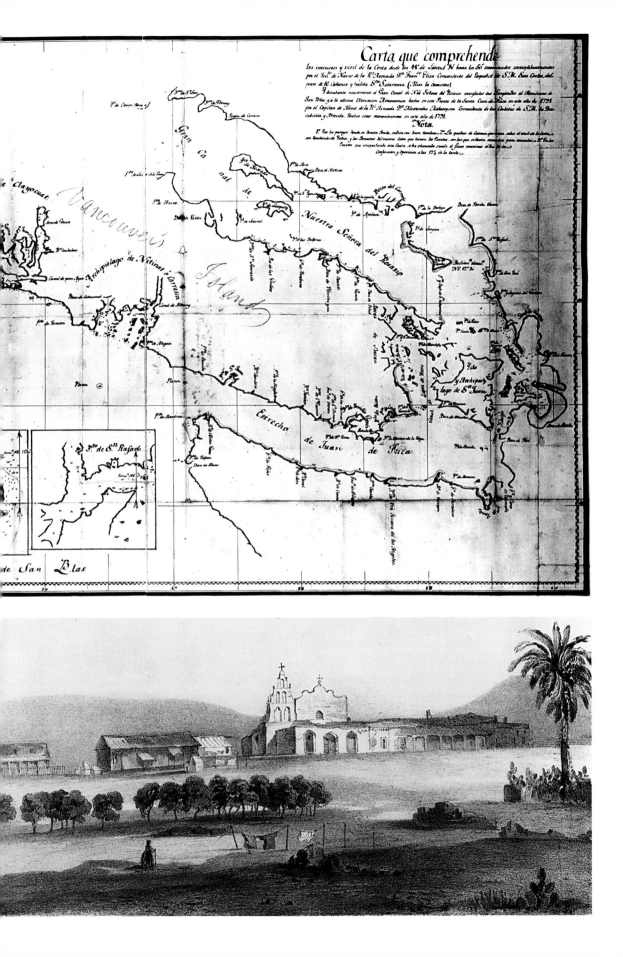

EXPLORING THE PACIFIC NORTHWEST

By the late eighteenth century, both America and Britain were interested in the northern Pacific Coast. An ocean expedition led by Captain James Cook had explored the northern coastline as early as 1778, finding Indian tribes who were willing to sell an abundance of valuable sea otter pelts. Upon learning of Cook's discovery, British fur merchants hurried west. The British government sent Captain George Vancouver to explore and map the Pacific coastline from San Diego to Alaska. He was the first person to sail around the island that today bears his name.

Reports of Captain Cook's expedition reached American explorers as well. Captain Robert Gray made his first voyage to the Pacific Northwest in 1787. On his second voyage, in 1791, he traveled along the coast in search of pelts and discovered the Columbia River. Several years later, Captain Ebenezer Dorr's ship, the *Otter*, became the first American ship to explore the California coastline. American and British fur traders would compete in the Pacific Northwest for the next fifty years.

British explorer Captain James Cook (1728–79; above) was a leading scientific explorer, using astronomy to make exact determinations of location. On his third Pacific voyage he discovered the Sandwich Islands (today's Hawaii). He mapped much of the North American Pacific coastline, traveling as far as the Arctic. He was killed by natives when he returned to Hawaii in 1779.

The discovery by Captain Robert Gray (1755–1806) of the Columbia River was the basis of the United States' claim to the Pacific Northwest. Traveling along the Pacific Coast, one of Gray's men noticed waves crashing over a bar. Gray investigated further and found himself at the mouth of the river. This illustration (opposite, bottom) depicts a craft similar to Gray's at the same spot.

Canadian explorer and fur trader Alexander Mackenzie (c. 1764–1820), shown in the center of the canoe in this painting by Frederic Remington, sought an easy route to the Pacific. After one unsuccessful attempt in 1789, he tried again in 1793, traveling West, first up the Peace River, then down the Fraser River. He followed Indian trails overland and finally reached the Pacific.

OVERLAND ROUTES TO THE PACIFIC

Because sea travel to the Pacific Northwest was expensive and time-consuming, British and American fur traders were anxious to find overland routes to the area. British explorer and fur trader Alexander Mackenzie made several attempts to find an overland route across Canada. He finally succeeded in 1793, traveling up the Peace River and spending the winter in the Canadian Rockies. Once across the mountains, he traveled down the Fraser River, which he mistook for the Columbia, and reached the Pacific in July 1793. He was the first white man to cross the continent north of Mexico.

American efforts were less successful. John Ledyard (1751–88), an American who had accompanied Captain Cook to the Pacific Northwest, was determined to return to the area to establish an American fur trading post. With the support of Thomas Jefferson, Ledyard proposed to travel across Russia, reach Alaska by sea, then travel south into the Pacific Northwest. He got no farther than Siberia, where he was arrested and deported. There would be no further efforts at overland expeditions into the area until Jefferson became president in 1800.

Fearful that British interests would try to claim the Pacific Northwest, Thomas Jefferson (1743–1826; above) asked frontiersman and soldier George Rogers Clark to undertake an expedition west. Clark did not accept. In 1792, Jefferson tried again to finance a westward expedition, this time by a French botanist. French political problems stopped the trip from going forward.

Native Americans (below) occupied most of the territory acquired by the United States from France in the Louisiana Purchase. Under French rule, land claims of Western Indian tribes were generally left unchallenged, but the wave of trappers, traders, and finally, settlers who followed the first American explorers West would push Western tribes off their ancestral lands permanently.

Part II: 1803–1835
The First Wave Across the Mississippi

William Clark (1770–1838) first served with Meriwether Lewis as an army corpsman on the frontier. His military experiences proved invaluable to him as co-commander of the Corps of Discovery. He was also responsible for mapping the journey.

In the early years of the nineteenth century, Americans moved eagerly across the Mississippi to explore the newly acquired Louisiana Territory and neighboring regions. It was the dream of Thomas Jefferson (1743–1826), as foreign minister to France, to undertake systematic and scientific studies of the West with an eye toward American settlement. At Jefferson's urging, Congress financed the Corps of Discovery, led by Meriwether Lewis (1774–1809) and William Clark (1770–1838), who spent more than two years exploring the Northwest. The Corps returned in 1806 with maps, journals, and plant and animal specimens. Later expeditions, however, were not as successful, and government enthusiasm for Western exploration faded.

Meanwhile, private enthusiasm grew, fanned by the demand for fur in Europe and in the East. Tales of a fur-rich West sent traders and trappers pouring across the Mississippi to scour the country for pelts. Traveling over unmarked territory and enduring incredible hardships, they soon became experts on the geography of the West. Tales of their adventures brought scientists, artists, and other explorers from Europe and the East. Guided by the trappers and traders, these visitors left a stunning written and pictorial record of the unspoiled West.

As sources of fur ran out, the trapping era quickly drew to a close. Most trappers came away with little but their ability to make their way through Western wilderness. This ability would prove quite valuable, however, to the next wave of Western explorers as the American government's interest in the West was rekindled.

UNITED STATES HISTORY

1803 The Louisiana Territory is purchased from France for $14.5 million.
•Washington, D.C., becomes the federal capital.

1804 Alexander Hamilton is killed in a duel with political opponent Aaron Burr in Weehawken, New Jersey.

1806 *A Compendious Dictionary of the English Language* is published by Noah Webster; it contains many words

Aaron Burr

unique to the American language that had not formerly appeared in British dictionaries.

1807 Former vice president Aaron Burr is tried for treason for his alleged involvement in a scheme to form a Western empire with the Spanish; he is acquitted, and leaves the country to avoid prosecution for the murder of Alexander Hamilton.
•The *Clermont* is built by Robert Fulton; it becomes the first commercially successful steamboat in the United States. On its maiden voyage, it travels up the Hudson River from New York City to Albany, New York, in thirty-two hours.
•The First African Presbyterian Church is established in Philadelphia.

1808 James Madison is elected the fourth president of the U.S.

1810 At age sixteen, Cornelius Vanderbilt begins building his transportation empire with a ferryboat service between New York City and Staten Island.

1812 Congress declares war against Britain on June 18, 1812.
•The U.S. warship

EXPLORING THE FRONTIER

1804 The Corps of Discovery, led by Meriwether Lewis and William Clark, leaves Camp Wood, near St. Louis, to explore the Western land acquired from France in the Louisiana Purchase.

1805 Sent to find the source of the Mississippi River, Lieutenant Zebulon Pike establishes Fort Snelling, the first American outpost in what is now Minnesota; he fails to find the source of the river.

•Late in the year, the Lewis and Clark expedition reaches the Pacific Ocean.

1806 On a second expedition, Zebulon Pike sights and explores the Rocky Mountains. On this journey he names Pikes Peak.
•The Lewis and Clark expedition returns to St. Louis on September 23. Many members of the expedition later return to the West as fur trappers.

1807 Sergeant Patrick Gass, of the Corps of Discovery, publishes his journal of the expedition.
•Fur trader Manuel Lisa leads a trapping expedition with John Colter up the Missouri River to what is now Montana.

Colter discovers the Yellowstone region.

1808 The St. Louis Missouri Fur Company is formed by explorers and traders such as William Clark, Manuel Lisa, and Pierre Chouteau.

Illustration from Patrick Gass's journal

Constitution ("Old Ironsides") scores a victory for the U.S. Navy by destroying the British frigate *Guerrière* on the St. Lawrence waterway.

1813 American forces capture York (now Toronto). The retreating British destroy their fort rather than let it fall into the hands of the Americans.

1814 Washington, D.C., is burned by the British. President Madison is forced to flee.

The fight between the Constitution *and the* Guerrière

•Francis Scott Key, an attorney, writes the famous "Star Spangled Banner" after the defeat of the British at Baltimore, Maryland.
•The Treaty of Ghent is signed on December 24, ending the War of 1812.

1818 The Convention of 1818 sets the border between the U.S. and Canada at the 49th parallel.

1820-21 Under the Missouri Compromise, Missouri is admitted to the Union as a slave state, and Maine is admitted as a free state. As a result, the balance between free and slave states is preserved.

1820 The New York Stock Exchange becomes the nation's leading stock exchange.
•The fourth census of the U.S. cites the nation's population at 10 million.

1821 The first public high school in the U.S. is established in Boston, Massachusetts.

1809 English botanist Thomas Nuttall explores the Missouri River through North Dakota.

1811 On a fur trapping expedition, Ezekiel Williams discovers the Colorado River. Most of the party are killed by Arapaho Indians.
•Canadian David Thompson becomes the first white explorer and geographer to travel from the source of the Columbia River to its mouth.
•Construction begins on the

Stephen Long

Cumberland Road; it eventually runs from Cumberland, Maryland, to Vandalia, Illinois.

1812 Robert Stuart crosses the continent from west to east using a route that becomes the Oregon Trail.

1814 The journals of Lewis and Clark are published.

1817 Geologist Henry R. Schoolcraft explores the area that is now Arkansas and southern Missouri. A few years later, he locates the source of the Mississippi River, in what is now Minnesota.

1819 An exploring party led by Major Stephen Long maps the Great Plains and climbs Pikes Peak, but fails to find the source of the Red River.

•Canadian explorer and fur trapper Donald McKenzie becomes the first white man to cross the portion of the Snake River known as Hell's Canyon.

1821 After Mexico wins its independence from Spain, traders begin to go west to Santa Fe to trade cloth and other manufactured goods for furs, mules, and silver. They become known as the Santa Fe Traders.

UNITED STATES HISTORY

1823 President James Monroe presents his Monroe Doctrine to Congress. In it he warns European nations not to interfere in the internal affairs of countries in the Western Hemisphere.

1824 John Quincy Adams is elected president by the U.S. House of Representatives when none of the other candidates wins a majority vote in the national election.

1825 The Erie Canal is completed; it runs from Lake Erie to the Hudson River at Albany, New York.

1826 Thomas Jefferson and John Adams die on the same day—July 4, 1826.

1828 Andrew Jackson becomes the seventh president of the U.S., defeating John Quincy Adams.

1830s Under the Indian Removal Act

The Erie Canal

of 1830, thousands of Cherokee, Seminole, Choctaw, Creek, and Chickasaw Indians are moved from their homes in Alabama, Tennessee, Georgia, and Mississippi to Oklahoma, in what is known as the Trail of Tears; 4,000 die en route.

EXPLORING THE FRONTIER

1822 Two important fur trading companies are formed: the Rocky Mountain Fur Company and the St. Louis branch of the American Fur Company.
•William Becknell, a Santa Fe Trader, crosses from Missouri to Santa Fe through the Cimarron Desert, creating the Santa Fe Trail.

1824 Explorer and fur trapper Jedediah Strong Smith leads an expedition through

Jim Bridger

the Dakota Badlands, the Black Hills, and the South Pass, in what is now Wyoming.

1825 Another explorer and fur trapper, Jim Bridger, is the first to report the discovery of the Great Salt Lake.
•The first "Rendezvous," in which fur trappers bring their year's catch to sell and trade for supplies, is held at the Green River, in what is now Wyoming.
•Peter Skene Ogden, Canadian explorer and fur trader, begins a journey on which he discovers the Humboldt River and finds a new

route to Mexico from the Pacific Northwest.
•Joseph C. Brown begins a two-year government-ordered survey of the Santa Fe Trail.

1826 Jedediah Smith and his expedition travel from east of the Great Salt Lake across the Mojave Desert to California. They are the first to use this route.

1827 On their way to California, Santa Fe Traders Sylvester Pattie and his son

1830 The nation's first regular steam railway service, with twenty-three miles of track, is opened to the public by the South Carolina Canal and Rail Road Company.

1831 Cyrus McCormick, an American inventor, develops the reaper, a harvesting machine, and revolutionizes farming in the U.S. and the world.

1832 Nominated by the newly formed Democratic Party,

Andrew Jackson is reelected president of the United States.

1833 *The New York Sun*, the first successful daily newspaper, is founded; an issue costs one penny.

1834 Abraham Lincoln enters politics for the first time, joining the assembly of the Illinois legislature; he is twenty-five years old.

1835 The national debt is completely

The first McCormick reaper

paid off as a result of revenues from increased railroad construction and skyrocketing land values.
•Mexico rejects the Texans' petition for statehood. When Mexicans try to dis-

arm the Texans in Gonzales, the Texans revolt. Texas organizes an army and appoints Sam Houston as its commander.

James Ohio Pattie sight the Grand Canyon.

1829 Mexican trader Antonio Armijo finds a new route from Santa Fe to California—the Old Spanish Trail.

1831 Kit Carson joins a fur trapping expedition with Mountain Man Thomas Fitzpatrick. He traps for the next ten years.
•Jedediah Strong Smith is killed by Comanche Indians on the Santa Fe Trail.

Prince Maximilian and Carl Bodmer

•Santa Fe Trader William Wolfskill is the first to take pack animals from Santa Fe to Los Angeles on the Old Spanish Trail.

1832 Benjamin Bonneville sets out for the Rockies with

explorer Joseph Walker to trap furs.

1833 German explorer and naturalist Prince Maximilian of Wied Nu-wied travels up the Missouri River, accompanied by artist Carl Bodmer.

•Joseph Walker and his party are the first white explorers to see the Yosemite Valley.

1834 An expedition led by Reverend Jason Lee, a missionary, explores the Willamette Valley, in what is now Oregon.

1835 The supply of furs in the Rockies begins to decline, as does the demand. The last Rendezvous is held five years later.

JEFFERSON PLANS TO EXPLORE THE WEST

Thomas Jefferson believed that exploring the West would yield important information about its natural wealth and political significance. Information of this kind would help to generate public support for the acquisition of Western territories. Explorers to the Northwest could report on the activities of British fur trading enterprises in the area and locate an overland route to the Pacific that American fur traders could use.

Soon after he was elected president in 1800, Jefferson planned an expedition to explore the West from the Mississippi River to the Pacific. In early 1803, Congress agreed to finance a small expedition. But once the Louisiana Territory was acquired through the Louisiana Purchase, the expedition took on national importance.

The president selected his secretary, Meriwether Lewis (1774–1809), to lead the expedition. Lewis had little formal education, but he had spent much of his youth exploring the wilderness and was an experienced frontier soldier.

Jefferson's interest in Western exploration went beyond the economic and the political. He was an avid student of the natural sciences and curious about the climate, soil, and plant and animal life of the West. To fulfill the scientific goals of the expedition, Lewis studied astronomy, medicine, and the natural sciences for months before assembling the party he would lead west.

This portrait of Meriwether Lewis (1774–1809; above) by Charles Saint-Memin was engraved shortly after Lewis returned from the West in 1806. Lewis's life following the expedition was marked by sadness. While serving as governor of the Missouri territory, he was plagued with political and financial problems that kept him from completing a story of the expedition to accompany Clark's maps.

The production of accurate maps of territory west of the Mississippi was an important goal of the Corps of Discovery. Earlier maps had been drawn by European cartographers based on the hearsay of French and Spanish soldiers. The maps produced by Clark, such as this one (opposite, bottom) for the Corps, would be used for years by the fur trappers and traders who followed in their footsteps.

This illustration (above) comes from an 1829 children's textbook, Interesting Events in the History of the United States. *It portrays a crisp, uniformed Corps of Discovery arriving at the shores of the Pacific Ocean. After a year and a half of travel through the wilderness, the Corps probably resembled bearded, buckskin-clad Kentucky Long Hunters.*

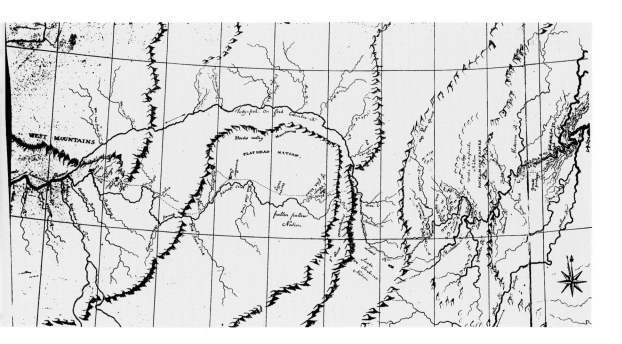

THE JOURNEY BEGINS

As his co-leader, Lewis chose William Clark (1770–1838), brother of George Rogers Clark. The two men had served together in the army, and Lewis had observed Clark's skills as a frontiersman. Clark's slave, York, knew several Indian dialects and became a valuable member of the expedition.

Lewis recruited the remaining members of the "Corps of Discovery" as he traveled west to prepare a winter camp near St. Louis. Corps members included American soldiers and frontiersmen such as John Colter, who remained in the West following the expedition. French fur trappers who could serve as translators were also enlisted. So were blacksmiths, carpenters, and other craftsmen whose skills would be required throughout the expedition.

After a difficult training process, a disciplined Corps of Discovery set out from St. Louis on May 14, 1804. They began their journey by traveling up the Missouri River in cumbersome boats laden with supplies, and were plagued by mosquitoes, bad weather, and the river's savage currents. Arriving near the site of present-day Bismark, North Dakota, they set up winter camp.

Sacajawea (c. 1787–c. 1812; opposite, top) belonged to the Snake tribe of the Shoshone Indians. As a girl, she was captured by the Minnetarees and taken east to what is now North Dakota. In 1804, she married a Canadian fur trapper living among the Minnetarees. The pair accompanied the Corps of Discovery as interpreters, providing an invaluable service.

Among the most valued members of the Corps of Discovery was York (below), the slave of William Clark. Besides his great physical strength and facility with Indian dialects, York brought vital diplomatic skills to the expedition. His manner often paved the way to peaceful relations with the tribes.

WEST TO
THE PACIFIC

Although the Corps had done little exploring on the way, they made peaceful contact with Indians and gathered plant, animal, and mineral specimens. The winter months were spent making maps and assembling information. They met up with Toussaint Charbonneau, a French trapper living among the Minnetarees, and learned that they would need horses for the journey that lay ahead. Charbonneau's wife, Sacajawea, a Shoshone who had been captured by the Minnetarees, could help purchase horses from her tribe farther west. Ultimately, Sacajawea and her husband joined the expedition.

When spring came, the party continued up the river. Carrying their canoes over treacherous bluffs at Great Falls in what is now Montana, they continued forward, catching sight of their first grizzly bears and bighorn sheep. Nearing the territory of Sacajawea's tribe, they floated down raging rivers and, on foot, crossed the Continental Divide on August 12, 1805. Nearby, they met Shoshone Indians and, with Sacajawea's assistance, purchased horses. They continued northward through the Bitterroot Valley, then headed west toward the Clearwater River. On October 16, they arrived at the Columbia River, following it into the Cascade Mountains. By November 7, they could see the Pacific Ocean. They set up winter quarters a few miles from the Pacific, knowing the westward leg of their journey had been accomplished.

This illustration (right), from the journal of a Corps of Discovery member, Patrick Gass, depicts a scene that was repeated often as the expedition navigated Western rivers. The rivers were full of swift currents, beaver dams, and other hazards that threatened constantly to capsize the canoes in which the party traveled.

After traveling for almost a year and a half, in October of 1805 the Lewis and Clark expedition reached the Columbia River, which led to the Pacific Ocean. In Frederic Remington's painting (below), the party is seen at the mouth of the river.

EAST FROM THE PACIFIC

The Corps of Discovery headed east along the Columbia River in March 1806. They returned to the Clearwater River to retrieve the horses they had left behind and traveled back to the Bitterroot Valley over the same Indian trail they had used the previous year. Lewis and nine men then crossed the Continental Divide by way of a pass in what is now Montana. This critical passage would later be known as the Lewis and Clark Pass.

Clark and his party, meanwhile, explored the Yellowstone River to its junction with the Missouri, where they rejoined Lewis's party on August 12, 1806. There, Sacajawea and her husband left the expedition. The rest of the party moved quickly down the Missouri River, and on September 23, 1806, they received a heroes' welcome in St. Louis.

Lewis and Clark accomplished much during their twenty-eight-month journey. Covering over 7,500 miles, often through unmapped territory, they proved that it was possible to reach the Pacific Northwest by land. Their notes on new species of plants and animals would aid scientists for years to come. Perhaps their most important contribution to the settlement of the American West was the detailed maps created by the expedition. It was these maps that would guide the traders and trappers who traveled west throughout the nineteenth century.

On the return journey, Lewis led a group of men to explore the area surrounding the Marias River, the territory of the Blackfoot tribe. When tribe members Lewis had invited back to camp tried to steal rifles and horses, fighting broke out (below), and Lewis shot one of the Indians. Fearing reprisals, Lewis quickly led his men out of the region.

THE PIKE EXPEDITION

Even before Lewis and Clark had returned, Jefferson sent more explorers West. In 1804, scientists William Dunbar and George Hunter were sent to investigate the Red River. Thomas Freeman, an astronomer and surveyor, was sent in 1806 to try the Red River again, but was turned back by Spanish soldiers.

In 1805, Lieutenant Zebulon Montgomery Pike led a party to locate the source of the Mississippi River. After mistakenly identifying Leech Lake, in what is now Minnesota, as the river's origin, he returned to St. Louis. Pike set out again in 1806, this time to explore the region between the Red and Arkansas rivers. He followed the Arkansas River to the Colorado Rockies, where he sighted and named (but did not climb) Pikes Peak.

On the return journey, Pike led his men into Spanish territory, where they were arrested. Spanish officials eventually released them in Mexico, but without the notes and maps they had made. Pike reconstructed most of the confiscated information and supplemented it with notes he made secretly as he was escorted from Mexico. With this data, he was able to publish a report that brought him popular acclaim. Congress, however, turned its attention to foreign policy problems that would result in the War of 1812, and government-sponsored explorations of the West were temporarily suspended.

Zebulon Montgomery Pike (1779–1813; above) began his military career as a frontier soldier. Two western exploratory missions made him a national hero. The first, in 1805, was to present-day Minnesota in search of the source of the Mississippi River. In 1806, Pike explored the Southwest, where he discovered and named Pikes Peak. Pike was killed in the War of 1812.

One of Pike's missions on his first expedition was to locate sites for forts. He selected as one of these sites the juncture of the Minnesota and the Mississippi rivers, near the Falls of St. Anthony (opposite, top). On September 23, 1805, he signed an agreement with the Sioux Indians, granting the United States nine square miles at the river junction.

In the winter of 1807, Pike and his men built a fort squarely within Spanish territory. Whether this act was purposeful or not, Pike was arrested by Spanish authorities (opposite, bottom). The arrest proved fortunate, as it enabled Pike to travel through the Spanish Southwest, normally closed to foreigners.

Frédéric Remington

EARLY FUR TRADERS AND TRAPPERS

Hearing reports from the Lewis and Clark expedition of a territory rich in beaver and game and clear of hostile Indians, traders and trappers flocked west. John Colter, a member of the Corps of Discovery, left the expedition early to stay in the West. Over the next several years, he traveled throughout the region that is now Wyoming and Montana and discovered many of the wonders of Yellowstone, including an area of thermal springs that became known as Colter's Hell. George Drouillard, who had also been with Lewis and Clark, returned west to trap and explore much of what is now Montana, including the Tongue and Bighorn river basins.

Manuel Lisa, a St. Louis merchant of Spanish descent, roamed the northern Rockies during the winter of 1807–08, and in 1811, Ezekiel Williams explored the valley of the North Platte River. Despite clashes with Indians who were alarmed by the invasion of their lands, trappers continued to pour across the Mississippi in ever-increasing numbers.

René Auguste Chouteau (1749–1829; left) and other St. Louis businessmen formed the Missouri Fur Company in 1807. They believed that large, well-supplied parties of trappers could defend themselves against hostilities of Western Indian tribes, while trapping enough furs to turn a profit. Chouteau participated in the company's first expedition to the Mandan villages in what is today North Dakota.

Over half the advance crew sent out by boat by the Pacific Fur Company to build a fort were killed. Some drowned, and others died when attacked by Indians. The overland party lost nineteen members en route. Several months later, the company surrendered Fort Astoria (below) to the British, who were then at war with the United States.

THE MOUNTAIN MEN

In the latter part of the fur trading era, the "Mountain Man" emerged in popular American lore. These men were solitary trappers who spent long months in the mountains searching for beaver pelts. Similar to the Long Hunters of the previous century, the Mountain Men roamed countless miles, learning intimately a geography that was alien to most Americans. Many went on to lead settlers west or to scout for the army. An observer, writing in 1847, said, "All this vast country...would even now be terra incognita [unknown land] to geographers...but there is not an acre that has not been passed and repassed by the trappers in their perilous excursions."

As more trappers went west, competition for pelts increased. Trappers penetrated remote areas to find pelts, heedless of the need to conserve the resource that provided their livelihood. By 1835, it was apparent that beaver were becoming scarce, and, by 1840, the West was nearly "trapped out."

This anonymous trapper (left) typifies the ideal Mountain Man. Like the Long Hunter before him, the Mountain Man needed few material goods. With little more than a rifle, traps, coffee, salt, and sugar, the Mountain Man could survive for a year as he roamed the Rockies in search of undiscovered areas to trap.

The landscape in this engraving (below) was meant to represent land over which fur trappers roamed. In reality, that land was far less tame. Trappers explored such sites as the Great Salt Lake, the Mojave Desert, and Yosemite Valley, among others.

ADVENTURES OF THE MOUNTAIN MEN

Many explorations made by Mountain Men were never documented, but those that were recorded were spectacular. Although others may have discovered it earlier, Jim Bridger (1804–98) was the first to report the Great Salt Lake. Bridger believed that the lake was a branch of the Pacific Ocean, but a later exploration proved him wrong.

David Jackson and William Sublette discovered the geysers of the Yellowstone region. Thomas "Broken Hand" Fitzpatrick led a trapping party through the South Pass of the Rockies to the unexplored Green River Valley. William Ashley rode the crashing rapids of the Green River in a canoe made of stretched buffalo hide and sticks. When at last he reached calm waters, he discovered a fur-rich area known as Brown's Hole.

After the fur trapping boom ended, trappers began to share their vast knowledge of the West. This knowledge was a great help in the American conquest of the West in the years ahead.

To escape from the prejudices of white society, many black Americans joined the rush of trappers to the Rockies. James Beckwourth (1798–c. 1867; above), whose mother was a slave, joined two trapping expeditions as a blacksmith, then chose to remain in the West. He married a member of the Crow tribe and eventually became a chief.

In 1906, Collier's magazine published a series of paintings by Frederic Remington of great North American explorers. Each painting featured an individual except for "The Unknown Explorers" (right) which honored the vast number of Mountain Men who explored miles of Western wilderness, but whose names are lost to history.

JEDEDIAH SMITH

Among the many traders and trappers in the West, several are considered truly great explorers. One of these is Jedediah Strong Smith (1799–1831). In 1822, Smith went west as an agent for the Rocky Mountain Fur Company and spent his first year exploring the Snake River. By 1826, Smith had begun to explore the Southwest. In that year, he led a party from the Great Salt Lake, across miles of desert in what is now Arizona, to reach California in November. These were the first Americans to travel overland to California. Smith left the coast by way of the San Joaquin Valley, crossed the Sierra Nevadas, and struggled across the Nevada desert. He reached the Great Salt Lake in 1827, having found a second overland route to California.

Smith soon returned to California by way of his original route. After being jailed by Mexican authorities, however, he attempted to leave by way of the Sacramento Valley. Unable to find a pass through the Sierras, he crossed the Coast Range mountains and eventually reached Oregon, returning to Wyoming in 1828. In 1830, he moved south to try his hand at the Santa Fe Trade, and was killed by Comanches on the Santa Fe Trail in 1831.

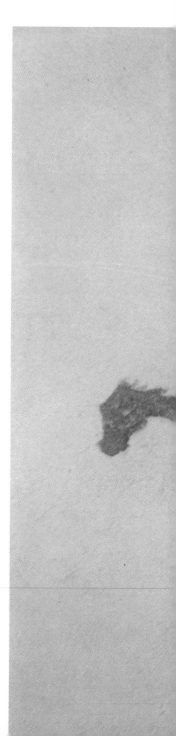

Frederic Remington's painting of Jedediah Strong Smith (1799–1831; below) leading his men across the Mojave Desert depicts a grueling episode from Smith's 1826 expedition to California. Smith and his men spent fifteen days crossing the desert, enduring blazing sun and chronic shortages of food and water, until, by trial and error, they reached Los Angeles.

CANADA COMPETES FOR FUR

Canadian and American fur companies were quick to recognize the wealth of furs in the Pacific Northwest. Canadian companies sent men to the region as early as 1800. Explorers and traders such as Finan McDonald and Duncan McGillivray wandered the Northwest in service of these companies, becoming experts on the geography of the area. The North West Company recruited David Thompson, astronomer and fur trader, to explore and map much of the territory around the northern Rockies.

In 1811, the Pacific Fur Company sent two expeditions, one by sea and the other by land, to establish a post in what is now Washington. The overland group, led by Wilson Price Hunt, did not follow the Lewis and Clark route because of Indian hostilities. Instead, they covered the Great Plains, crossing the Continental Divide by way of a new pass along the Wind River. Following the treacherous Snake River, they reached the new company post in early 1812. In 1813, Robert Stuart led a small group east to report on the company's progress. In a harrowing journey, the party discovered the South Pass through the Rockies, then followed the Platte River east, establishing a route that would become the famous Oregon Trail.

Peter Skene Ogden (1794–1854; above) had a reputation as a quick-tempered, violent man. This led his superiors in the Hudson's Bay Company to send him into the wilderness, away from the company's Fort Vancouver headquarters. For years he headed the company's annual expedition to the Snake River, and, eventually came to present-day southern Idaho and eastern Oregon.

In 1821, two major Canadian fur companies, the North West and the Hudson's Bay, joined forces against the American fur trappers who were beginning to invade their territory. This merger joined the best scouts and explorers of both companies. The vision of the partnership is captured in the engraving below.

JOSEPH REDDEFORD WALKER

Joseph Reddeford Walker moved west in 1818 and eventually traveled to Santa Fe. There he trapped and traded for several years and assisted the United States government survey of the Santa Fe Trail. In 1832, he became the field commander for a fur trapping expedition led by Benjamin Bonneville. Exploring the Salmon and Snake rivers, the expedition yielded little in the way of furs but much in the way of information.

In 1833, Walker organized an expedition to California. Following his own instincts as well as the advice of local Indians, Walker devised a route that would eventually become part of the transcontinental railroad. This route took Walker along the Humboldt River and across northern Nevada. When the members of the expedition crossed the Sierras, they became the first Americans to cross from east to west. While in California, they explored the Yosemite region, then returned through the Sierras by a newly discovered pass (Walker's Pass). Walker spent the rest of his life in the West, successfully guiding settlers, soldiers, and prospectors through the difficult territory until he was nearly blind.

Mystery surrounds the role of Benjamin Bonneville (1796–1878; above) in the history of Western exploration. Officially, he took a two-year leave from the army to trap in the Rockies, but many believe he left active service to gather information on Western territory not yet in American hands. In any case, he was not a successful trapper, but did, with Joseph Walker's help, learn much about the geography of the Far West.

This painting by Alfred Jacob Miller of Joseph Walker (1798–1876; right) portrays Walker at a Rendezvous of Mountain Men in the 1830s. Among his fellow trappers, Walker's trailblazing abilities were legendary. He also had a reputation as a fair, capable leader whose careful preparations minimized the danger of wilderness travel.

THE SOUTHWEST AND SANTA FE TRADE

In late 1821, William Becknell was on his way from St. Louis to the Colorado Rockies with fabrics, metal tools, and other manufactured goods to trade for furs trapped by the Indians. When he learned of Mexico's newly won independence, he changed his plans and rushed to Santa Fe, where he sold his wares at a tremendous profit. On his second trip to Santa Fe, he followed the Arkansas River and crossed the Cimarron Desert. This route became the famous Santa Fe Trail.

Sylvester Pattie headed west in 1824 with his son, James Ohio Pattie. When plans to trap along the Missouri River fell through, they turned south into Mexico's territory. Over the next several years, the Patties explored and trapped in the areas surrounding the Gila and Colorado rivers, following the Colorado River to its source in the Colorado Rockies. They were the first Americans to sight the Grand Canyon. In 1827, they crossed the Mojave Desert, discovering a new overland route to California.

In 1830, American traders William Wolfskill and Ewing Young marked a trail to California that became known as the Old Spanish Trail. Upon reaching Los Angeles, Young remained in California, exploring and trapping in the San Joaquin and Sacramento valleys.

This illustration (right) was published in the Personal Narrative of James Ohio Pattie of Kentucky, written when Pattie (1804– c. 1850) returned to Kentucky from California. He described in colorful detail his adventures and geographical discoveries. Although the authenticity of portions of the journal is questionable, the volume is one of the few firsthand accounts of early American exploration of the Southwest.

Santa Fe (below) was settled by the Spanish in about 1610. Under Spanish rule, the town grew to about 2,000 inhabitants whose main exports were furs, silver, and mules. In the early 1800s, American explorers began to make their way to the Southwest, many hoping to find trade outlets or trapping opportunities.

STEPHEN LONG'S EXPEDITION

Following the War of 1812, the American government's interest in Western exploration increased. Two expeditions were sent west under Major Stephen Long. The first reached no farther than the site of present-day Omaha, Nebraska.

In 1820, Long's second expedition set out to find the source of the Red River. They traveled up the Platte River to the Rockies, where three expedition members became the first white men to climb Pikes Peak. The party then moved south to the Arkansas River, where they explored the Royal Gorge. Long took half the expedition across the Purgatory and Cimarron rivers while the other half continued on the Arkansas River. Long's party mistook the Canadian River for the Red and followed it back to the Arkansas, where they realized their mistake.

Like others before him, Long failed to find the source of the Red River. But the scientists, the artist, and the topographer (mapmaker) who accompanied him brought back useful information. Long himself mapped a large part of the Great Plains, producing the most scientifically accurate Western map of his day.

Like Zebulon Pike before him, Stephen Long (1784–1864; above) labeled the Great Plains the "Great American Desert," dimming official interest in further exploration of the region. In 1823, Long's last expedition brought him to the Great Lakes to locate sources of the St. Peter's (now Minnesota) River and the northern boundary of the United States.

Many of the notes and maps from Stephen Long's trek to the Rockies were lost. However, British artist Samuel Seymour, who accompanied Long, painted and sketched what he saw and managed to leave a valuable visual record of the journey. Seymour's "Distant View of the Rockies" (opposite, top) gave the American public its first glimpse of the magnitude of the mountains.

In 1819, Long commanded part of an expedition to explore the Yellowstone region. Before leaving, Long arranged a meeting with the Pawnee tribe. This engraving (right) is based on a drawing by Samuel Seymour.

SCIENTISTS BRAVE THE WEST

Scientific observations made by Lewis and Clark and other early explorers caught the attention of European and American scientists. Many went west themselves for a firsthand look. Most scientists adapted easily to frontier living conditions, to the astonishment of the fur trappers with whom they frequently traveled. The information they brought back was a great enhancement to American understanding of the West.

English botanists Thomas Nuttall and John Bradbury were the first trained scientists in the West. They accompanied Wilson Price Hunt up the Missouri River in 1810, then continued west with Manuel Lisa. Nuttall remained in the West for five years and gathered enough material to publish *Genera of North American Plants*, still considered a masterpiece. In 1834, he returned to the West with American ornithologist John Kirk Townsend. The pair discovered several types of birds that were previously unknown to the scientific community.

Scientists also made geographic discoveries that had eluded explorers for years. Over the next fifty years, trained scientists sent west by the United States government would build on the foundations laid by these pioneer scientists.

English scientist Thomas Nuttall (1786–1859; above) had little in common with the seasoned frontiersmen who traveled with him on his first trip up the Missouri River. But Nuttall stood up well to the dangers of wilderness travel, collecting thousands of plant, animal, and mineral specimens along the way.

Nuttall traveled throughout the United States studying natural history. Though he was primarily a botanist, he collected animal specimens as well and even discovered several new types of birds. Some of these bear his name—the Phalaenoptilus nuttalli, *a type of whippoorwill, for example. This page (right) is from Nuttall's A Popular Handbook of the Ornithology of Eastern North America.*

PI.X.

1. Ruby-Throated Hummingbird.   4. Whip-Poor-Will.
2. Barn Swallow.   5. Cardinal.
3. Flicker.   6. Red-Headed Woodpecker.

EUROPEAN
EXPLORERS
IN THE
AMERICAN WEST

Reports of adventure, natural wonders, and new plant and animal species in the American West spread quickly abroad, luring explorers from far beyond American borders. British explorers Frederick Ruxton and William Drummond Stewart traveled throughout the West in the company of Mountain Men. Frederick Paul Wilhelm, Duke of Wurttemburg, left Germany in 1822 for a journey which took him up the Missouri River, through the Yellowstone region, to Texas, California, and the Rockies.

Prince Alexander Philip Maximilian of the German principality of Wied Nuwied sailed for North America in 1832. Prince Maximilian came to study the flora and fauna and the Indian tribes of the American West. He set out from St. Louis, having read reports of other Western travelers and having talked to scientists, artists, and explorers who preceded him.

Along the way, Prince Maximilian collected thousands of scientific specimens and Indian artifacts. Among his most valuable contributions to the knowledge of the West was his thorough study of the Mandan tribe, which was wiped out by smallpox several years later. His meticulous notes and the paintings of his companion, artist Carl Bodmer, provided Americans and Europeans with a written and pictorial record that captured Western life at a period in which little was recorded by American explorers.

Prince Maximilian (1782–1867) traveled with the American Fur Company because of its good relations with Western Indian tribes. While in the West, he came to know the Mandan, Hidatsa, and Blackfoot tribes. Prince Maximilian recorded his observations in journals, even illustrating them as seen on this page, which shows a buffalo robe with a battle scene.

JOHN C. FREMONT.

Wᴹ L. DAYTON.

THE REPUBLICANS CHOICE FOR PRESIDENT AND VICE PRESIDENT FROM 1857 TO 1861.

Entered according to Act of Congress in the Year 1856 by N.Currier, in the Clerk's Office of the District Court of the Southern Dist of N.Y.

GRAND NATIONAL REPUBLICAN BANNER.

FREE LABOR, FREE SPEECH, FREE TERITORY.

LITH.& PUB. BY N.CURRIER 152 NASSAU St. N.Y.

Part III: 1836–1900
Charting Challenging Territory

John C. Frémont (1813–90) was one of the most visible and vocal supporters of nineteenth-century Westward expansion. Following several exploratory expeditions to the West, Frémont was elected to the Senate from the California territory in 1849. He was defeated by proslavery forces when he sought a second term. This poster is from his unsuccessful presidential campaign of 1856.

As settlers continued to move west in the late 1830s, the idea of American territorial expansion began to gain public support. This support blossomed into the notion of "Manifest Destiny"—the idea that the spread of American democracy to the Pacific was divinely ordained. Fur trappers and traders had explored the West thoroughly but left little in the way of formal records of their travels. If the West was to be united under an American flag, it needed to be mapped and surveyed. Boundaries and transportation routes had to be established; fertile land and mineral resources needed to be identified. The Army's Corps of Topographical Engineers was chosen to carry out these tasks.

Enduring the same hardships as the trappers and traders, Corps members combed the West, studying not only the topography, but also the Indian customs and the plant and animal life. The consolidated reports of the various expeditions conducted by the Corps provided the first scientific study of the West.

The "Great Surveys," carried out in the 1870s, were among the last official exploratory expeditions in the West. Photographs of spectacular Western scenery helped convince the American public that parts of the West should be saved from commercial exploitation. As the nineteenth century ended, President Theodore Roosevelt (1858–1919) was among those who fought to conserve the West's natural resources. Today, environmental organizations continue the fight to preserve America's rich physical resources and natural beauty.

The Army Corps of Topographical Engineers led the American government's most serious efforts to explore the West in the 1840s. On their early expeditions, the Corps sometimes crossed into foreign territory, bringing back information on settlement possibilities and natural resources. During the Mexican War, members of the Corps were also sent to the Southwest with combat troops to map and assemble information on disputed territory. Once the war was over, the Corps marked the new boundary. Army engineers also mapped the Canadian border.

In 1853, after all territorial acquisitions of the continental United States were complete, plans for a transcontinental railroad began. Four paths were mapped across the West as engineers searched for a feasible route. Although the building did not begin for more than ten years, the reports from these surveys provided accurate maps, as well as a complete natural history of the regions they covered.

By the late 1860s, the federal government was sponsoring explorations of Western territory from the Great Plains to the Pacific, to fill in any gaps left by the earlier surveys. Civilian scientists headed most of these exploring teams. They scoured their assigned areas, studying plant and animal life, mineral deposits, and many of the remaining Western Indian cultures. These explorers were followed by American settlers who were drawn to the West by photographs taken during these expeditions.

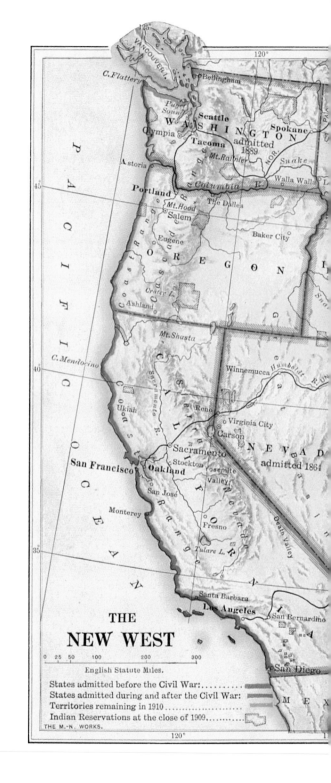

THE

NEW WEST

0 25 50   100   200   300

English Statute Miles.

States admitted before the Civil War:..........
States admitted during and after the Civil War:
Territories remaining in 1910......................
Indian Reservations at the close of 1909...........
THE M.-N. WORKS.

UNITED STATES HISTORY

1836 Mexican general Antonio López de Santa Anna leads a force of 3,000 soldiers against 187 Texans at the Alamo, killing all within the garrison.
•Texans declare their independence and elect Sam Houston president.

1845 The House of Representatives and the Senate adopt a joint resolution calling for the annexation of Texas.

1846 Mexican forces cross the Rio Grande and skirmish with U.S. troops. The U.S. declares war against Mexico.

1848 The U.S. and Mexico sign the Treaty of Guadalupe-Hidalgo, ending the Mexican War.

1853 James Gadsden, U.S. minister to Mexico, negotiates the Gadsden Purchase, in which the U.S. acquires 29,640 square miles of land for $15 million. Later the price is reduced to $10 million.

1858 Abraham Lincoln meets Senator Stephen Douglas in a series of seven senatorial debates about the slavery issue. Lincoln gains national attention as an antislavery spokesman.

1860 Lincoln defeats Douglas in the presidential election, despite his lack of support in the slave states.

1861 Seceding states form a new Southern union called the Confederate States of America.
•The U.S. Civil War begins when South Carolina's forces fire on Fort Sumter, near Charleston, South Carolina.

1862 Over 10,000 people are killed at the Battle of Antietam on the bloodiest day of the war.

1863 Lincoln frees all slaves in seceding states when

EXPLORING THE FRONTIER

1836 The Corps of Topographical Engineers is founded; its members include important explorers of the middle and late nineteenth century.

1839 Joseph Nicollet follows the Red River to its source; he also explores the area of Devil's Lake in North Dakota.

1840 Artist George Catlin returns to the East with more than 500 paintings of Indians and Western subjects; these paintings provide an important record of the changing West.

1842 With Kit Carson as his guide, John C. Frémont leads an expedition to map the Wind River Range, in present-day Wyoming.

1843 Artist John Audubon travels up the Missouri River to collect specimens for his book on North American animals.

1846 Under the leadership of Brigham Young, thousands of Mormons leave Illinois in search of religious freedom; they settle in the Salt Lake Basin in 1847.

1848 The first accurate map of the Southwest is published in a report by Lieutenant William Emory of the Corps of Topographical Engineers.

1850 Indian cliff dwellings are discovered in Navajo territory at Canyon de Chelly by an expedition led by Lieutenant James Hervey Simpson, in what is now Arizona.

1853 Government-sponsored surveys are initiated to find the best Western route for a transcontinental railroad.

1864 President Abraham Lincoln grants to California an area to be used by the public as a state park; the area

he issues the Emancipation Proclamation.

1864 Confederate general Robert E. Lee surrenders to Union general Ulysses S. Grant at Appomattox Courthouse in Virginia, ending the Civil War. •President Lincoln is assassinated by Southern patriot John Wilkes Booth.

1866 Congress passes the Civil Rights Bill of 1866, granting full citizenship to all people born on U.S. soil.

1869 The Wyoming Territory passes the first law in the U.S. giving women the right to vote.

1877 The last federal troops stationed in the South are withdrawn from New Orleans, and the Southern states regain control of their governments.

1887 Congress passes the Dawes Act, which divides Indian reservation land into plots of 160 acres; the extra land is opened to white settlers.

Totem of the Sioux Indians

1889 The U.S. government allows white settlers to claim land in Oklahoma which had formally been given to the Indians.

1890 U.S. troops massacre 200 Sioux Indians at the Battle of Wounded Knee, in South Dakota.

1896 The Supreme Court rules in *Plessy* v. *Ferguson* that "separate but equal" facilities for blacks and whites are constitutional.

1900 The Foraker Act confirms Puerto Rico as a territory of the U.S.

---

includes the Mariposa Grove of Big Trees and the Yosemite Valley.

1866 James T. Evans discovers the Lone Tree Pass, which is critical to the Union Pacific leg of the transcontinental railroad.

1870 Henry Washburn, Nathaniel Langford, and Lieutenant Gustavus Doane explore the Yellowstone region.

1871 Lieutenant George M. Wheeler, as part of a federal

survey project, leads an expedition up the Colorado River to map and survey the general area of Nevada.

1872 Congress creates Yellowstone Park in Wyoming to help conserve the

Wheeler's exploring party

nation's endangered natural resources.

1874 Ferdinand Hayden finds dwellings from an ancient Indian civilization in the Mancos Canyon, in Colorado.

1879 The U.S. Geological Survey is established, with Clarence King as its first director; he is succeeded by John Wesley Powell in 1881.

1892 The Sierra Club is founded with the help of naturalist John Muir. Initially formed to fight the destruction of forests, its members later help create the National Park Service.

OFFICIAL EXPLORATION BEGINS

The decline of the fur trade did not mean a decline of American interest in the West. Americans were becoming secure in the belief that the West would and should be settled by Americans. The United States Army's Corps of Topographical Engineers, formed in 1838, would help make that belief a reality.

Corps members were recruited from among the brightest engineering graduates of West Point. They were originally sent west to survey areas to which infantry and cavalry would be sent, but their tasks grew to include marking the United States borders with Mexico and Canada, mapping trails for settlers and postal routes, and surveying potential railroad routes. The territory they surveyed was often uninhabited, and conditions under which the Corps worked were not much better than those endured by the Mountain Men.

Using horizontal and vertical measurements and mathematical calculations, surveyors can accurately determine the form and position of a piece of land. But Corps surveys went beyond this technical process. With artists, geologists, anthropologists, and botanists on the surveying teams, these surveys produced reports that were broad in scope. They offered not only accurate maps, but an illustrated natural history of the West.

Joseph Nicholas Nicollet (1786–1843), a French mathematician and astronomer, came to the United States in 1832. He settled in St. Louis, where the Chouteau family encouraged him to map and survey Western regions. This 1839 map (right) shows Nicollet's course down the Mississippi from a port near Fort Snelling to the St. Croix River.

This engraving (below) is an illustration from a multivolume report prepared by Lieutenant Charles Wilkes (1798–1877) on the expedition that took him to the Pacific Northwest. His was primarily a sea voyage, but some members of the expedition traveled overland from Vancouver to San Francisco, in part to strengthen American claims to the region.

JOHN C. FRÉMONT

The most famous member of the Corps of Topographical Engineers is probably John C. Frémont. Frémont, a mathematician, was the son-in-law of Senator Thomas Hart Benton, an ardent proponent of Westward expansion. Frémont began his career assisting Corps explorer Jean Nicollet and, by 1842, was in command of an expedition that mapped the Green and Wind rivers and the South Pass of the Rockies.

In 1843, on an expedition that was designed to find a route to Oregon, Frémont covered almost the entire West. After exploring much of the Rockies and the Wasatch Mountains, he led the expedition to the Columbia River, then along the Des Chutes River to what is now Nevada. There he identified and explored the Great Basin, a depression in the land that extends over a vast area in present-day Nevada and Utah. He then led his men on a grueling trek across the Sierras in the middle of winter. They recuperated in California before heading east by a southern route with Mountain Man Joseph Walker as their guide. On their way, they explored the South Park in what is now Colorado, as well as the Arkansas and Purgatory rivers.

NARRATIVE

OF

THE EXPLORING EXPEDITION

TO

THE ROCKY MOUNTAINS,

IN THE YEAR 1842;

AND TO

OREGON AND NORTH CALIFORNIA,

IN THE YEARS 1843-44.

BY

BREVET CAPT. J. C. FREMONT,

OF THE TOPOGRAPHICAL ENGINEERS,

UNDER THE ORDERS OF COL. J. J. ABERT, CHIEF OF TOP. BUREAU

SYRACUSE:

PUBLISHED BY HALL & DICKSON.

NEW YORK:—A. S. BARNES & CO.

1847.

Jessie Frémont shaped her husband's narratives of Western treks into readable reports that elevated him and Kit Carson to the status of national heroes. The reports, which often emphasized Frémont's own adventures at the expense of the men who served under him, generated popular support for Westward expansion. This title page (above) is from the report on two of his early treks.

In 1842, John C. Frémont survived one of his most daring exploits—climbing a peak of the Wyoming Rockies and planting a flag at the summit (opposite, top). The climb was dangerous, the party was ill-equipped, and the feat produced little in terms of increased geographic knowledge. Nevertheless, it earned Frémont the admiration of the American public.

Daughter of a senator from Missouri, Jessie Benton (1824–1902; right) was a well-educated young woman from Washington, D.C., when she met and married John C. Frémont. Although she never accompanied him on his expeditions, she was as enthusiastic as her husband about Westward expansion. Her skill as a writer helped publicize his accomplishments.

FRÉMONT AND KIT CARSON

Glowing accounts of Frémont's explorations, prepared by Frémont and his wife, Jessie Benton Frémont, were widely read and helped turn public attention to the West. In these accounts, Frémont gave much of the credit for his success to his guide, Kit Carson (1809–68). Born in Kentucky, Carson was raised on the Missouri frontier, where he received no formal education. As an adult, he headed into the Southwest to trap with Ewing Young, exploring much of California and Arizona in the process. He then headed north to the Rockies and trapped and explored with Jim Bridger and Thomas Fitzpatrick. After acting as Frémont's guide, Carson scouted for the army in California, fought in the Indian wars, and became U.S. agent for the Ute tribe. And Frémont's cartographer (mapmaker), Charles Preuss, helped him produce a scientifically accurate map of the West.

Frémont's next expedition took him to the Southwest. In 1845, he crossed over into California, where he became involved in California's revolt against Mexico. While in California, Frémont was court-martialed and found guilty of disobedience. His sentence was suspended by President James K. Polk, and Frémont returned to his exploration of the West. Later he entered politics, becoming California's first governor and the first presidential nominee of the newly formed Republican Party in 1856.

After Christopher "Kit" Carson (1809–68; right) left Frémont's service, he participated in the Mexican War and in numerous battles with Southwestern Indians. In spite of the fact that he could neither read nor write, Carson was appointed U.S. Indian agent for the Ute tribe in 1853. Nevertheless, he was able to dictate reports and correspondence and served well in that position.

Carson left his Missouri home for Santa Fe before he was twenty. In the Southwest, he quickly adapted to frontier life and roamed as far as California and Montana to trap. This wood engraving by F. O. C. Darly (below) depicts Carson in a scene typical of the fur trapping era.

OTHER CORPS EXPLORERS

In addition to Frémont, several other official explorers made equally important contributions to American knowledge of the West. In 1838, under the command of Captain Charles Wilkes, the six ships of the United States Exploring Expedition traveled around the Pacific to explore Australia and Antarctica before heading for the Pacific Northwest. There, Wilkes and his men made a thorough study of the coastline north of the Columbia River while searching for a usable harbor. Some of his men also made a trip inland and explored the area that is now Oregon and Washington.

An early explorer for the Corps of Topographical Engineers, Jean Nicollet (1786–1843) explored and surveyed the upper Missouri River, Devil's Lake in what is now North Dakota, and the source of the Red River. During the Mexican War, Corps surveyor Lieutenant William Emory accompanied soldiers to Santa Fe and then traveled west to California by way of the Gila River and the Mojave Desert. Emory's report of this journey contained the first accurate map of the Southwest. He was one of the first to urge conservation of the West's natural resources.

The Corps of Topographical Engineers did not ignore the Indian groups they encountered along the way. This lithograph (above) appeared in Captain Randolph B. Marcy's report of his 1852 expedition to the Red River. This illustration and others like it are often the only recorded firsthand observations of some Western Indian tribes.

Many survey topographers were also talented artists who painted and sketched scenes of Western Indian life. This lithograph of Mariano Martinez (opposite, top), a Navajo leader, is taken from a drawing by Edward M. Kern, a topographer for the 1849 Simpson survey of the Southwest.

F. W. von Egloffstein, a skilled German topographer for the Joseph C. Ives expedition to the Grand Canyon, provided illustrations for the Ives survey report that captured the grandeur of the region. This lithograph (right), made near the Grand Canyon, uses the tiny human figures in the foreground to illustrate the vastness of the territory.

SCHOOLCRAFT AND EASTMAN

During the mid-1800s, several expeditions were launched to study the Indian tribes of that area. In 1819, American geologist Henry Schoolcraft began exploring the area that now includes Michigan, Minnesota, and Wisconsin. On his first expedition he became interested in the Indian tribes of the region, and by 1822 he was appointed Indian agent for the tribes of Lake Superior. He continued to travel among the tribes—studying Indian customs, languages, and religions—and made important geographical discoveries along the way. In 1832, he finally located the source of the Mississippi, a lake in present-day Minnesota which he named Itasca.

Schoolcraft wrote extensively about his explorations, both officially and unofficially. His writings culminated in a six-volume history of the Indian tribes of the United States, which was illustrated by U. S. Army officer Seth Eastman. Eastman had little formal training as an artist, but his paintings of Indian subjects had attracted favorable attention. Both Eastman and his wife, a writer, were enthusiastic students of Indian languages and culture, particularly of the Sioux tribe. Eastman's paintings of American Indians, noted for their accuracy and detail, are valuable both artistically and historically. He was one of the few painters to concentrate on scenes from the daily lives of Indians.

INQUIRIES,

RESPECTING THE

HISTORY, PRESENT CONDITION,

AND

FUTURE PROSPECTS,

OF THE

Indian Tribes of the United States.

BY HENRY R. SCHOOLCRAFT,
OFFICE INDIAN AFFAIRS,
WASHINGTON, D. C.

PHILADELPHIA:
LIPPINCOTT, GRAMBO & CO., PUBLISHERS.
1851.

While investigating the geology of the Upper Mississippi and Lake Superior regions in 1820, scientist Henry Rowe Schoolcraft (1793–1864) began his study of the area's Indian tribes (above). He served as Indian agent for the tribes of Lake Superior and later as Michigan's superintendent of Indian affairs.

As a result of his service in the West, Seth Eastman (1808–75) developed a profound interest in Western Indian groups, particularly the Santee Sioux. He learned Indian languages and painted scores of scenes of Indian daily life (opposite, top). Among his work are 300 illustrations for Henry Schoolcraft's six-volume history of Indians in the United States.

Eastman, an engineer and army officer with little artistic training, painted throughout his military career. He served seven years on the frontier, many of them in present-day Minnesota at Fort Snelling (right). His paintings are valued today both as historical documents and works of art.

MORE SCIENTIFIC EXPLORATIONS OF THE WEST

Important discoveries were made in the West during and following the railroad surveys. Exploring New Mexico's Canyon de Chelly for the first time since Spanish explorers in the seventeenth century, Lieutenant James Hervey Simpson (1813–83) came upon cliff dwellings of a lost Indian civilization. An expedition in 1857–58, led by Lieutenant Joseph Christmas Ives, explored the Grand Canyon. John Strong Newberry, a geologist accompanying the Ives expedition, published an important record of the different layers of earth in the Grand Canyon. Mapmaker F. W. von Egloffstein, also part of the Ives expedition, drew the first relief map of the West.

During an expedition in western Colorado in 1859, Captain John Macomb discovered the junction of the Green and Grand Rivers, which explorers had been trying to find for years. That same year Captain William F. Raynolds combed the Dakota Badlands and unearthed the remains of extinct animal species. Maps contained in the official reports of these and other expeditions were combined on one map by Lieutenant Gouverneur K. Warren. This map became one of the most important documents produced by Western explorers.

Isaac Ingalls Stevens (1816–62; right) embarked on the task of surveying the proposed northern railroad route just after he was appointed governor of the newly created Washington Territory. The route he surveyed began at Fort Snelling and ended at Puget Sound in the Washington Territory. Not surprisingly, Stevens concluded in his report that his route should be selected for the railroad.

Surveying is a painstaking process in which distances are measured using calculations that account for the curvature of the earth's surface. In this lithograph (below), surveyors of a railroad route set up a level on a tripod, a telescope-like instrument through which measurements are made between two points.

THE GREAT
SURVEYS

Western exploration was sharply cut back during the Civil War. But once the war was over, the federal government financed a series of expeditions that would become known as the "Great Surveys." These surveys, which took place in the 1870s, filled in the few remaining blanks on the map of the American West, and provided a comprehensive list of Western resources.

The first surveyor was Ferdinand Vandiver Hayden. A doctor by training, he was far more interested in studying fossils and rock formations than in medicine. He had explored the West for a number of years before receiving a Congressional grant to survey the easternmost region covered by the Great Surveys. One of the many regions covered in his survey was Yellowstone. Impressed by its natural wonders, he urged that it be preserved as a park. Out of Hayden's careful mapping of the Colorado Rockies came his classic *Atlas of Colorado*.

Clarence King was the next to begin his survey. King had studied the natural sciences in college and had worked on a geological survey of California. His survey covered the area through which the transcontinental railroad eventually passed. His team studied the plant and animal life of the area and, of greatest interest at the time, its mineral resources. At Mount Shasta, King proved many other scientists wrong when he discovered that active glaciers did exist in the United States.

Clarence King (1842–1901; above) made a name for himself in scientific circles after participating in the California Geological Survey. He was appointed to head the U.S. government survey of the 40th parallel when he was only twenty-five. King is pictured here in one of his team's mountain camps.

This natural column (opposite, top), in present-day Wyoming, was first sighted by the Clarence King expedition in 1870. King persuaded Congress to finance the survey by arguing the expedition would assess the vast mineral wealth believed to reside in the uncharted West.

Ferdinand Hayden (1829–87) was appointed by the U. S. Department of the Interior to undertake a major Western survey in 1870. He assembled an impressive corps (right) to accompany him to a region that included much of present-day Montana and Wyoming. His survey report was optimistic about the economic potential of the West.

POWELL AND WHEELER

John Wesley Powell, a geologist, had lost an arm in the Civil War, but still undertook dangerous expeditions in the Southwest. He climbed a high peak in the Rockies to prove that the network of rivers that drained into the Colorado River could provide a water passage from the Rockies to the Pacific. He later explored many of those rivers, including the Colorado, which runs through the Grand Canyon.

Congress financed a survey by Powell of the region through which the Colorado River ran. This region, which Powell called the Colorado Plateau, included parts of the present-day states of Arizona, New Mexico, Utah, and Nevada. Through his study of the area, Powell and his colleagues were able to show how the plateau was created. Like other explorers before him, Powell stressed in his survey report the need for restraint in settling the Southwest, to conserve its limited water and timber resources.

Lieutenant George Montague Wheeler led the last of the Great Surveys. Wheeler, the only military surveyor, had graduated from West Point and joined the Corps of Topographical Engineers. He spent three years mapping and surveying the Great Basin before he led the last of the Great Surveys. The survey produced spectacular maps of the West, in addition to detailed studies of the Grand Canyon and the mining areas in Nevada known as the Comstock Lode.

The canoe was a life-saving form of transportation for Western explorers. Lightweight and easy to build, the canoe enabled explorers to cross unanticipated rivers and streams. This photo (right), taken by John Wesley Powell in the Colorado River Valley, is titled simply, "Our Boats."

The deep gorges of the Colorado River (below) had fascinated and terrified Western explorers for years, but the river was not explored thoroughly until Powell and Wheeler surveyed the region. Although Powell made two trips down the river before him, Wheeler took his team up the river in what he described as a test of the limits of navigation.

5

Timothy O'Sullivan, a photographer trained during the Civil War, was one of the best known survey photographers. He shot this photograph (above) of his darkroom wagon as the King survey team crossed the Carson Desert in Nevada. He later joined the Wheeler survey, making a series of photographs of the lands of Southwest Indian tribes.

Technological advances in the 1860s enabled photographers to accompany surveyors to document the natural beauty of the West (right). But by no means did these advances make outdoor photography easy. Photographers had to battle weather hazards and cope with cumbersome developing techniques with nothing more than a tent or a wagon for a darkroom.

SAVING WHAT
THE EXPLORERS
HAD FOUND

The wonders of Wyoming's Yellowstone region had fascinated explorers. In 1870, civilians Nathaniel Langford and Henry D. Washburn, with a military escort led by Lieutenant Gustavus Doane, combed the area, mapping it and identifying its wonders. Their work was completed the next year by Captain John Whitney Barlow. Participants in both expeditions petitioned Congress to declare Yellowstone a national park, which it did in 1872.

By the late nineteenth century, many people were convinced that other parts of the West had to be saved. Laws were passed to control the use of timber and water in areas where they were scarce. Through the efforts of naturalist John Muir, California's Yosemite Park was enlarged and made into a national park in 1890. Private groups such as the Boone and Crockett Club, founded in 1888 by Theodore Roosevelt, and the Sierra Club, founded in 1892 by Muir, urged that other areas be set aside as parks and wildlife refuges. As a result, Olympia, Zion, Mount Rainier, and other national parks were created, and the National Park Service was formed. These efforts preserved portions of the West that would otherwise be known only to history.

Naturalist John Muir (1838–1914; above) emigrated to the United States from Scotland when he was a boy. He spent six years studying the Yosemite Valley, eventually proving that glaciers had formed the valley through erosion. He was an ardent conservationist, and his efforts were responsible for the establishment of Yosemite and Sequoia national parks.

Theodore Roosevelt (1858–1919; opposite, top) had a lifelong interest in preserving the beauty and natural resources of the West. He wrote extensively about the region and traveled widely in the Northwest. His most lasting achievement occurred during his presidency, when vast amounts of land were set aside as national parks, and many conservation measures were initiated.

The majestic scenery of the Yosemite Valley (right) captured the attention of the American public. The name "Yosemite" means grizzly bear and refers to the totem, or symbol, of the Indian group that once occupied the area.

Resource Guide

Key to picture positions: (T) top, (C) center, (B) bottom; and in combinations: (TL) top left, (TC) top center, (TR) top right, (BL) bottom left, (BC) bottom center, (BR) bottom right.

Key to picture locations within the Library of Congress collections (and where available, photo negative numbers): P - Prints and Photographs; HABS -

Historical American Buildings Survey (div. of Prints and Photographs); R - Rare Book Division; G - General Collections; MSS - Manuscript Division; G&M - Geography and Map Division.

PICTURES IN THIS VOLUME

2-3 Yosemite Valley, P 4-5 Toad, G 6-7 Mountains, P

Part I: 8-9 Boone, P 10-11 Map G 12-13 TL, Jones, P, USZ62-45184; BL, Boone, P; TR, West Point, G 14-15 TL, Gist, G; BC, canoe, P 16-17 TR, house, P, USZ62-47562; BR, plan, P, USZ62-30702 18-19 BL, rifle, G; TR, camp, P; BR, Kenton, P, USZ62-077027 20-21 TL, Finley, G; TR, Robertson, R 22-23 TL, Boone, P, USZ62-7493; BR, Indian, P, USZ62-1431 24-25 TL, title page, R; BR, Indians, P, USZ62-8107 26-27 TC, map, P, USZ62-7282; BR, mission, P, USZ62-10000 28-29 TL, Cook, P, USZ62-25351; TR, MacKenzie, G; BR, boat, P, USZ62-31249 30-31 TL, Jefferson, P; BR, Indians, G

Part II: 32-33 Clark, P 34-35 TL, Burr, G; BL, woodcut, P, USZ62-17371; TR, ships, G; BR, Long G 36-37 TL, canal, G; BL, Bridger, P, USZ62-02623; TR, reaper, G; BR, Maximilian, R 38-39 TL, Lewis, P; TR, soldiers, G; BR, map, G&M 40-41 BC, York, R; TR, Sacajawea, R 42-43 TR, boat, P, USZ62-19232; BR, Lewis and Clark, P, USZ62-50631 44-45 C, men w/guns, P, USZ62-19231 46-47 TL, Pike, P, USZ62-19731; TR, falls, P, USZ62-31877; BR, town, P, USZ62-50630 48-49 TL, Chouteau, P, USZ62-42561; BC, fort, P, USZ62-17656 50-51 TL, Mountain Man,

P, USZ62-63405; BC, forest, P 52-53 TL, Beckwourth, R; TR, explorers, G 54-55 C, Smith, G; TL, Ogden, P, USZ62-059793; BR, boats, P, USZ62-10517 58-59 Bonneville, R; TR, Walker, G 60-61 BC, Santa Fe, P, USZ62-17606; TR, Pattie, R 62-63 TL, Pike, P, USZ62-2616; TR, landscape, G; BR, Indians, P, USZ62-7778 64-65 TL, Nuttall, P, USZ62-7656; TR, birds, G 66-67 C, journal page, G

Part III: 68-69 Poster, P 70-71 Map, G 72-73 TR, totem, G; BR, Wheeler, P, USZ62-22311 74-75 BC, camp, P, USZ62-8110; TR, map, G&M 76-77 TL, title page, MSS; TR, Frémont, P, USZ62-049597; BR, Benton, P, USZ62-44060 78-79 BC, trappers, P, USZ62-870; TR, Carson, P, USZ62-1371 80-81 TL, village, P, USZ62-11478; TR, Martinez, P, USZ62-46898; BR, canyon, R 82-83 TL, title page, MSS; TR, canoe, P, USA7-34115; BR, fort, P, USZ62-24901 84-85 BC, surveying, P, USZ62-35766; TR, Stevens, P, USZ62-19726 86-87 TL, King, P, USZ62-42767; TR, column, G; BR, camp, P, USZ62-052437 88-89 BC, river, P, USZ62-048448; TR, boat, P, USZ62-23850 90-91 TC, desert, P, USZ62-22290; BR, photographer, P, USZ62-22309 92-93 TL, Muir, P, USZ62-25974; TR, Roosevelt, P, USZ62-091139; BR, Yosemite, P

SUGGESTED READING

AMERICAN HERITAGE. *Trappers and Mountain Men.* Mahwah, New Jersey: Troll Associates, 1961.

ANDRIST, RALPH K. *To the Pacific with Lewis and Clark.* New York: American Heritage Publishing Co. Inc., 1967.

DANIEL, CLIFTON. *Chronicle of America.* New York: Prentice Hall, 1989.

JOSEPHY, ALVIN M., JR. *The World Almanac of the*

American West. New York: Pharos Books, 1986.

McGRATH, PATRICK. *The Lewis and Clark Expedition.* New York: Silver Burdett, 1985.

MORRISON, SAMUEL E. *The Oxford History of the American People.* New York: Oxford University Press, 1965.

TIME-LIFE. *The Trailblazers.* New York: Time-Life Books, 1973.

Index

Page numbers in *italics* indicate illustrations

Appalachian Mountains, 9,
  10,18, 20
Arkansas River, 46, 60, 62, 76
army
  See Corps of Discovery; Corps
  of Topographical Engineers
Ashley, William, 52

Barlow, John Whitney, 92
Becknell, William, 60
Beckwourth, James, *52*
Bighorn River, 48
Bitterroot Valley, 42, 44
Blacks, 40, *40-41*, *52*
Bodmer, Carl, 66
Bonneville, Benjamin, *58*
Boone, Daniel, *8*, 9, 18, 21,
  22, *23*
Bradbury, John, 64
Bridger, Jim, 52, 78
Britain, 14, 28, 38

California, 24, *25*, 26, *27*, 28,
  54, 58, 60, 78, 86
Canada, 10, 14, 30, 56, *57*,
  70, 74
Carson, Kit, 76, 78, *78-79*
Cascade Mountains, 42
Champlain, Samuel de, 14
Charbonneau, Toussaint, 42
Chouteau, Auguste, 16
Chouteau, Rene Auguste, *48*, 49
Cimarron Desert, 60
Cimarron River, 62
Clark, George Rogers, 20, 30, 40
Clark, William, *32*, 33, 40
Clearwater River, 42, 44
Coast Range Mountains, 54
Colorado, 10, 76, 86, 88
Colorado River, 60, 88, *88-89*
Colter, John, 40, 44, 48
Columbia River, 28, *29*, 42,
  43, 44, 80
Comstock Lode, 88
Continental Divide, 42, 44, 56
Cook, James, 28
Coropa Mountains, 26
Corps of Discovery, 33, 38, *39*
  40, *40-41*, 44
Corps of Topographical
  Engineers, 69, 70, 74, 76,
  80, 88
Cumberland Gap, *8*, 9, 22
Cumberland River, 20, 21
Cumberland River Valley, 22
Cutbird, Benjamin, 20

Darley, F.O.C., *7*, 79
De Anza, Juan Bautista, 26
Des Chutes River, 76
De Soto, Hernando, 16
Devil's Lake, 80

Doane, Gustavus, 92
Dorr, Ebenezer, 28
Drouillard, George, 48
Dunbar, William, 46

Eastman, Seth, 82
Egloffstein, F. W. von, 80, 84
Eliza, Francisco, 26
Emory, William, 80
explorers/expeditions
  in California, 24, 26, 28, 78,
    86
  European, 66, 67
  of Frémont, 76, 78
  fur trade and, 28, 30, 33,
    48, *48-49*, 56
  of Long, 62, *63*
  in Northwest, 14, *14-15*
  in Pacific Northwest, 28, *29*, 39
  of Pike, *46*, 47
  scientific, 46, 64, *65*, 66, 70,
    84
  in Southwest, 16, *17*, 60,
    60-61
  surveyors, 15, 58, 69, 70,
    74, 80, 84, *84-85*
  of traders/trappers, 18,
    19, *20*, 21, 22, *50*, 51, 52,
    53, 54, 55,58
  See also Lewis and Clark
    expedition

Falls of St. Anthony, 46
Finley, John, *20*, 21, 22
Fitzpatrick, Thomas, 52, 78
Florida, 10, 16
Fort Astoria, *48-49*, 49
Fort Crevecoeur, 14
Fort Snelling, 82, *83*
Fort Vancouver, 56
France, 14, 16, 31
Fraser River, 29, 30
Frémont, Jessie Benton, 76,
  77, 78
Frémont, John C., *68*, 69, 76,
  77, 78
fur traders/trappers, 14, 15, 16
  Long Hunters, 18, *19*, 21, 22
  Mountain Men in, *50*, 51, 52,
    53, 58, *59*
  in West, 28, 30, 33, 48, *48-49*,
    50

Galvez, Jose de, 24
Garces, Francisco, 26
Gass, Patrick, 42
Gila River, 60, 80
Gist, Christoper, 15
Grand Canyon, 60, 80, *81*, 84,
  88
Grand River, 60, 85
Gray, Robert, 28

Great Basin, 76, 88
Great Falls, 42
Great Lakes region, 14
Great Salt Lake, 52, 54
Green River, 52, 76, 84
Green River Valley, 20, 22, 52

Hayden, Ferdinand Vandiveer,
  86
Hudson's Bay Company, 15, 56,
  57
Humboldt River, 58
Hunter, George, 46
Hunt, Wilson Price, 56, 64

Indians, 10, *25*, *31*, 82, *83*
  and fur trade, 16, 48, 49
  and Lewis and Clark
    expedition, 40, *40-41*,
    42, 44, *44-45*, 45
  studies of, 66, *66-67*, 80,
    80-81, 82, 88
  trails, 22, 29, 44
Itasca Lake, 82
Ives, Joseph Christmas, 84

Jackson, David, 52
Jefferson, Thomas, 10, *30*, 33,
  38, 46
Jolliet, Louis, 14

Kenton, Simon, 18, *19*, 20
Kentucky, 8, 10, 15, 16, 18,
  20, 22
Kentucky River, 22
King, Clarence, *86*
Knox, James, 20

Laclede, Pierre, 16
Langford, Nathaniel, 92
La Salle, Rene Robert de, 14
Ledyard, John, 30
Leech Lake, 46
Lewis and Clark expedition
  Corps of Discovery in, 33,
    40, *40-41*, 44
  and Indians, 40, *40-41*, 42,
    44, *44-45*, 45
  Jefferson and, 33, 38
  maps of, 38, *39*
  return journey of, 44, *44-45*
  route of, 42
Lewis, Meriwether, 33, *38*, 44,
  45
Lisa, Manuel, 48, 64
Long, Stephen, *62*
Louisiana Purchase, 10, 31, 38
Louisiana Territory, 31, 33,
  38

McDonald, Finan, 56

McGillivray, Duncan, 56
MacKenzie, Alexander, *29*, 30
Macomb, John, 84
Malaspina, Alejandro, 26
Marais River, 45
Marcy, Randolph B., 80
Marquette, Jacques, 14
Martinez, Mariano, 80
Maximilian, Prince, 66, 67
Mexico, 24, 26, 46, 60, 74, 78
Miller, Alfred Jacob, 58
Minnesota River, 62
missions, 24, *25*, 26, 27
Mississippi River, 10, 14, 16,
    17, 20, 38, 46, 64, 82
Missouri Fur Company, 49
Missouri River, 40, 44, 60,
    62, 64, 66, 80
Mojave Desert, 60, 80
Monterey Bay, 24
Moran, Thomas, 6
Mountain Men, *50*, 51, 52, *53*,
    58, *59*
Muir, John, *92*

national parks, 92
Newberry, John Strong, 84
New Orleans, 20
Nicollet, Joseph Nicholas, 74,
    76, 80
North Platte River, 48
North West Company, 56, 57
Nuttall, Thomas, *64*

Ogden, Peter Skene, *56*
Ohio, 10, 14, 18
Ohio River, 15, 20
Old Spanish Trail, 60
Oregon, 54, 80
Oregon Trail, 56
O'Sullivan, Timothy, 88

Pacific Fur Company, 49, 56
Pacific Northwest
    fur trade in, 48, *48-49*, 49, 56,
        57
    overland routes to, 29, 38,
        39, 42
    sea travel to, 28, *29*
Pacific Ocean, *39*, 42
parks and wildlife refuges, 92
Pattie, James Ohio, 60, *61*

Pattie, Sylvester, 60, *61*
Peace River, 29, 30
Pikes Peak, 46, 62
Pike, Zebulon M., *46*, *47*
Platte River, 56, 62
Polk, James K., 78
Ponce de Leon, Juan, 16
Portolá, Gaspar de, 24
Powell, John Wesley, 88
Preuss, Charles, 78
Purgatory River, 62, 76

Radisson, Pierre Esprit, *14-15*,
    15
railroad, transcontinental,
    58, 70
Raton Pass, 60
Raynolds, William F., 84
Red River, 22, 46, 62, 80
Remington, Frederic, 29, 42,
    52
rifles, flintlock, *18*
Robertson, James, 20, *21*
Rocky Mountains, 30, 46, 60,
    62, *63*, 76, 78, 86
South Pass, 52, 56, 76
Roosevelt, Theodore, 69, 92,
    93
Royal Gorge, 62
Russia, 24, 25, 30
Ruxton, Frederick, 66

Sacramento Valley, 54, 60
Sacajawea, 40, *41*, 44
St. Louis, 14, 16, *17*, 40, 44,
    60
Saint-Memin, *7*, 38
Salmon River, 58
San Diego, 24
San Francisco Bay, 24
San Gabriel Mission, 26
San Jacinto Mountains, 26
San Joaquin Valley, 54, 60
Santa Fe, 60, *60-61*, 80
Santa Fe Trail, 54, 58, 60
Santa Lucia Mountains, 24
Schoolcraft, Henry, 64, 82
Scientific expeditions, 46,
    64, *65*, 66, 70, 84
Serra, Junípero, 24
Seymour, Samuel, 62
Sierra Nevada, *6*, 54, 58

Simpson, James Hervey, 84
Smith, Jedediah, 54, *55*
Smoky Mountains, 20
Snake River, 54, 56, 58
Spain, 10, 16, *17*, 24, 26, *27*,
    46, 60, *60-61*
Stevens, Isaac Ingalls, 84, *85*
Stoner, Mike, 20
Stuart, John, 20
Stuart, Robert, 56
Sublette, William, 52
surveyors/surveying, 15, 58, 69,
    70, 74, 80, 84, *84-85*, 86,
    87, 88, *88-89*, 90, *90-91*

Tennessee, 10, 16, 18, 20
Texas, 10
Thompson, David, 56
Tongue River, 48
Townsend, John Kirk, 64
Trail, Santa Fe, 54, 58, 60
trappers
    See fur traders/trappers
Treaty of Versailles, 10

Utah, 76, 88

Vancouver, George, 28
Vicksburg (Nogales), 16, *17*

Walker, Joseph Reddeford, 58,
    59, 76
War of 1812, 46
Warren, Gouverneur K., 84
Warriors' Path, 22
Wasatch Mountains, 76
Washburn, Henry D., 92
Washington, 56, 80
Wheeler, George Montague, 88
Wilkes, Charles, 74, 80
Williams, Bill, 78
Williams, Ezekiel, 48
Wind River, 56, 76
Wisconsin, 14, 15
Wolfskill, William, 60
Wurttemburg, Paul Duke of, 66
Wyoming, 48, 54, 86, *87*

Yellowstone region, 48, 52,
    62, 66, 86, 92
Yellowstone River, 44
York (slave), 40, *40-41*
Yosemite region, 58, 92, *93*